ESSENCE *of*
Beaufort
& THE LOWCOUNTRY

Essence of Beaufort
& The Lowcounty

A community-supported, cooperative effort by and for the people of Beaufort County to benefit youth and the environment.

BOYS & GIRLS CLUB

This book is being marketed and distributed through a youth entrepreneurial partnership at the Boys & Girls Club of Beaufort.

Compiled by Caryl Sweet

KC Newnham & Company
Beaufort, South Carolina

Book and Cover Design
by Kelly Newnham and Caryl Sweet

Published by
KC Newnham & Company
170 Gannet Point Road
Beaufort, South Carolina 29902

ISBN 0-9674200-0-8
Library of Congress Catalog Card Number: 99-90865

Acknowledgments

Essence of Beaufort is a community-supported, cooperative effort. I am indebted to many people and organizations for their cooperation, talents, moral support, and financial aid.

Senior Leadership Beaufort, 1998, inspired an environmental project. Anne Pearson of the Alliance for Sustainable Communities in Annapolis, MD contributed a copy of Orion Afield (Spring 1998) which contained an article by Betsy Teter (Hub City Writers). It was that article along with a phone call to Betsy that launched this book.

Area writers and artists, amateur and professional, were invited to contribute a piece of their work expressing a personal perspective about Beaufort County. There were numerous responses and contributions were accepted with the promise that they would only be used for this book and any associated publicity. All other rights remain with the contributors.

Beaufort County Public Schools were all invited to participate. To our delight, Beaufort Academy asked to be included. The following schools submitted work and at least one piece of their students' work is included in this publication: Battery Creek High School, Beaufort Academy, Beaufort Elementary School, Beaufort High School, Broad River Elementary School, James J. Davis Elementary School, Hilton Head High School, Humanities School of Beaufort, Michael C. Riley Elementary School, Lady's Island Middle School, Mossy Oaks Elementary School, Penn Center's PACE Program, St. Helena Elementary School, and Shell Point Elementary School.

Initial and ongoing support was provided by USC Beaufort's Continuing Education Department through its Director, Dr. Harriett Hilton who helped us secure seed money from Arts Council of Beaufort County. She also obtained permission from the University to provide the design and printing of our first brochure as well as support of her office staff, equipment and materials. Dr. Hilton promoted the book at every opportunity and brought in many valued contributions. In addition, Megan Dannenfeldt, Robert Cuttino, Martin Goodman, Mark Polombo, Al Hefner & Marlys West, at USC Beaufort, assisted and advised to help launch the project.

Eric Holowacz, Director of Arts Council of Beaufort county advised on the preparation of a funding proposal, and on organizing and implementing other phases of the project. He also provided valuable connections with artists, writers, and funding sources.

At Eric's suggestion we recruited an Advisory Board to help identify "holes" in the book and to guide us through the process of publishing, and marketing. Advisors include: Ralph Bailey, Grayco; Heather Bosworth, W.D Bosworth Woodworking; Emory S. Campbell, Penn Center; Barbara Catenaci, Beaufort County Schools Community Development; Henry Chambers, Beaufort Realty; Glen McCasky, Del Webb's Sun City Hilton Head; Warren Dickson, Friends of Hunting Island; Jane Frederick, FMF Architects; John Heath, Beaufort Gazette; Irene Hoogenboom , Environments and Boombears Toy Store; Billy Keyserling, Keyserling Realty; Stan Lawson, Ace Basin Tours, Inc; Robert A. Marshall; Joseph Mix, Island Outfitters; Michael Murphy, Preservation Tree Care; Tom Peeples, Mayor of Hilton Head; Anna Pinckney, Port Royal Historic Foundation; Tony Royal, Bay Street Outfitters; J. Wood Rutter, Beaufort Academy; Col Lawrence Staak, MCAS; Christine Stanley, Bay Street Trading Co.; John Webber, Economic Director, Beaufort County; O.C. Welch , O.C. Welch Ford Co; Thomas D. Wilson, Beaufort County Planning.

An Editorial Team was selected to create the look and feel we wanted for the book. Margaret Holly, Brewster Robertson and Jim Sweet edited the initial contributions. Sheila Tombe Ellen Malphrus, Bob Louttit, Warren Dickson, and Eric Holowacz took successive turns editing and proof-reading to make the final manuscript as near perfect as possible. Arianne King Comer of Ibile Indigo House, gave artistic and technical advice, and Will Cook helped with layout and design.

Kelly Newnham joined the team when the project was ready for a professional graphic artist. She patiently and expertly collaborated with me to develop a logo and to make the book camera-ready for the printer. Irene Hoogenboom, of Boombears Toy Store, was especially helpful in showing us how to improve the design and marketability of the book. Helen Harvey, Gregg Shorey, Barbara Pinkerton, Christine Stanley and Fran Marscher generously gave of their time and professional advice as it was needed. Dan Morgan at the County Planning Office gave us their latest map for inclusion in the book, and a collaborative effort between The Beaufort County Library and The Beaufort Artists Association provided display space for the public to view the book in progress.

In the eleventh hour, I decided to offer the proceeds of the book to the Boys and Girls Club of Beaufort if they would market and distribute it. At my request, Joe Mix arranged a meeting with Mark Branch and Stephanie Edwards and I presented my idea. An ingenious entrepreneurial partnership evolved that gives youth a learning opportunity as they help manage the project. I am delighted with this turn of events and am confident that the Boys and Girls Club will make the very best of their opportunity.

The following persons made contributions ranging from $100 to $12,000 to cover the cost of publication. Without their generous support this book could not have been printed. Persons whose names are followed by an asterisk donated books to contributing students.

GUARDIAN ANGELS

Carl and Sylvia Ziegler*

GUARDIANS

Mr. & Mrs. Sumner Pingree
Reasoning, Inc.*
Jesse & Dele Schaudies
Dick & Sharon Stewart

SUPPORTERS

Athena Corporation*
Boombears Toy Store*
E. John Daugs
Mr. & Mrs Henry C. Kocmond
Townsend F. MacCoun
George & Jean Morgan
Tom & Dottie Oliver
Renaissance Communities
Edie Rodgers
Seaway Development Corporation
Diane Terni
Triangle Ice & Gas

SPONSORS

Betty & Michael Adams
Joe Adams
Barbara Aimar
Sandra & Jack Baggette
John & Ann Ballantyne
Gardner Bandfield
Arthur & Marcia Baron
Donnie Ann Beer
Mr. & Mrs. William W. Bonneville
Carolyn Enloe Bremer
Vic & Nancy Brinkman
Pete & Nancy Cameron
James J. Chaffin, Jr.
Mr. & Mrs. Thomas Clark
Fran & Bill Cobb
Hildred Fern Collier
Wanda Cook
Brent & Dianne Cooper
Glenn Cooper
Melba Cooper
Martha Crapse
Marj & Allan Dehls
Del Webb's Sun City Hilton Head
Warren and Mary Dickson*
Norma P. Duncan
Stephanie Edwards
Barbara Jean Eskridge
Sally, Amy, Amanda,& Duncan Fordham
FMF Architechts
John & Ella Fox
Friends of Hunting Island*

Harriette E. Gause
D.C. Gilley, Jr.
Malcom & Susan Goodridge
Mr. & Mrs. G.A. Grande
Jonathan Green
Mimi & Steve Greenberger
Candace Grose
Bob Guinn
Owen Hand
Bob & Judy Harnsberger
Annelore Harrell
Evelyn C. Hartzog
Mr. & Mrs. Brantley Harvey
Joan & John Hedley
Mr. & Mrs. Raymond Hein
Harriet Hilton
Sharon & Dan Hopkins
Theotis & Claudette Humphrey
Ibile Indigo House
Island Outfitters
Lynn Jerdsild
Mr. & Mrs Russell J. Jeter
Mr. & Mrs. J. Gwyn Jordan
Ron & Carrol Kay, Two Suns Inn
Harriet Keyserling
William Keyserling
Julian S. Levin, PA
Anne & Bob Louttit
Mr. & Mrs. Christopher MacMurray
Paul & Sue Mannheim
Mr. & Mrs. Guy McSweeney
Mr. & Mrs. Joseph A. Mix
Vicki & Steve Mix
Eugene C. Mowry, Jr.
Michael Murphy
Kathleen Myrick
Mrs. Frankie Nelson

Chris & Kelly Newnham
J. Eugene Norris
Mr. & Mrs. Michael G. O'Neill
Bill and Josie Paddock
Patterson Realty
Emmett & Sarah Polk Paul
Town of Port Royal
Peter & Jane Post
Alton & Betty Powell
Roy & Mary Reed
Michael & Corrine Reeves
Sarah Tavener Reynolds & James F. Reynolds, Jr.
Brewster Robertson
William C. Robinson, CPA
Charles & Collette Russell
Penny & Dave Russell
J. Wood Rutter
Dr. & Mrs. Russell J. Sacco, MD
Emma R. Sanders
Letty Lee Saville
Mr. & Mrs. Francois Seguin
Carolyn Smith
Floyd D. Spence
Caryl & Jim Sweet*
Jim & Stacey Sweet
John & Joan Templer
Landon & Missy Thorne
Billy & Sally Timms
Trask & Potter
Frank & Barbara Tuckwiller
John & Jennifer Tuckwiller
W.R. VonHarten
Mrs. Robert Wardle
Richard A. Warner
Mr. & Mrs. David Zebley
Loren & Rusty Zimmerman
Fred & Dorothy Zinser

Shalonda Bryan 11th Grade - Beaufort High School

Table of Contents

List of Illustrations

Foreword

Here is what the essence of Beaufort is to me: no matter
where else I am on earth, I always hear Beaufort
calling my name. Once I lived in a sixteenth century house
in Rome, Italy and kept writing love letters to the creeks
and marshes of Beaufort, South Carolina.
I collected these letters and named them *The Prince of Tides*.

Later, I would live in an apartment next to the Piazza
Farnese in Rome, then moved to a house in Brookwood Hills
in Atlanta, then on to a house in San Francisco overlooking the
Golden Gate Bridge. Beaufort hunted me down at every stop,
stalked me in my waking hours, and haunted me
from midnight to dawn. The love letters to Beaufort kept
pouring out of me, but this time I called them *Beach Music*.

All the people in this book know what I am talking about.

Pat Conroy

Jonathan Green

Three Steps of Beaufort

Here we have a unique place
Where we know our direction
The steps, they number three
But after the last, one must leave
Never to forget what he has seen.

The first step is the original
Uncharted adventure island, reachable
only by boat.
There you anchor: fiddler crabs run
To their own sanctuary
Within, the trees rise high and heavy.
Kingfishers build their nests here,
Thriving on the jumping mullet, caught
In a deep, aquatic hole, unaware of falling tides.
The scenery almost unchanged for years.
Untamed, untainted marsh.
Wise, oak satyrs; bluffs along the rivers
Clear, ethereal sunsets, always changing color.

The second step shows buildings of old
Some so rustic, but so beautiful.
Stately Antebellum homes; spirit of the South
Heart of history.
Pensive railroad tracks, leading to unknown

townships as they always have.
Downtown, the old commerce that everyone
loves to remember: family run hardware stores,
Banks, clothing shops and pharmacies.
Forts of past turmoil, graveyards of forgotten
Unknown soldiers, shaded by a strangely
perfectly placed palmetto.
Adjacent to the highway that was once dirt
Only traversed by horse and foot,
But now leading to the third step.

Stretching out with the tides of culture
Homogenization, the modern part of Beaufort
Hustle and Bustle, sales, bright lights, noise.
But you wanted this.
Entertainment is everywhere, even in the traffic.
Which moves you forward the next
Step that hasn't come to be yet,
But is sure to come...
Here we had a unique place
Where we knew our direction
The steps, they numbered three.
But after the last, one had to leave,
Never to forget what he had seen.

Brandon Cooper, 10th Grade - Beaufort Academy

While I Slept

While I slept
A mother loggerhead
Tracked her way onto Edisto beach
A silhouette
Barely visible in wet darkness.

While I slept
Predetermined and intent
She dug her cache.

Flashes of light
Distant thunder
Electrified the birthing ritual.

One by one eggs
rolled into their place
packing 150 into the nest.

She covered her eggs,
Patted the ground
A million times
Over a million years.

While I slept,
She tracked her path back to the sea
Pushing aside wet sand
Ridges rising as evidence
Of her disappearing presence

While I slept
The surf moved in
Erasing
Lapping near
The sandy womb
Where her babies nested.

While I slept
They slept.

Melba Cooper

Melba Cooper

The Marsh

The beautiful marsh
Is home for all things
Fir land creatures and water creatures
It vanishes at high tide
And appears at low tide
And never goes away.

The marsh is where the egret bathes
It is where the gators come to feed.
It tickles the fish's colorful fins

And protects the nest of the sea gulls.
The wind blows the marsh this way and that
And yet never seems to be blown away

The marsh is the pelican's home
It is where their young ones grow.
It is always the most peaceful place
On the face of the earth

Bekah Bowen, 7th Grade - Beaufort Academy

Moss

Moss, Oh Moss
    How do you hang
      From a tree?
Do you jump on a tree?
Do you climb up a tree? Or
Do you walk up a tree?
    How did you get on a tree?
Do you get a rope?
Grab a branch or limb,
And climb it up?
    How did you get on a tree?
How did you? How did you?

Shaquetta Ruth, 5th Grade
James J. Davis Elementary

Eric Horan

"I'm a Raccoon"

I'm a Raccoon
I eat eggs.

What do you eat, Chicken,
Chicken?

I'm a Raccoon,
I eat baby alligators too.

What do you eat, Chicken,
Chicken?

I'm a Chicken
I eat worms,

What do you eat, Raccoon?

You. Chicken!

Marrion Jarrell Chisolm, 5th Grade
James J. Davis Elementary

Barbara LaPlante

6

Lowcountry Sky

The Lowcountry sky is filled with warm
golden tones,
soft pinks and coral hues
mixed together like a watercolor dream.
The heart of this tranquil scene
peeking out from the earth's other side:
the sun.

Air rushes over the water
as if it has somewhere to go
though it doesn't.
It slips like fingers through
my hair
the wind. The soft soil sinks beneath
my feet

and the water delicately tickles
my toes.
The musty smell of pluff mud
fills my nostrils and...
marsh grass sways to form
intricate patterns which
appear and disappear in seconds:
the marsh.

I hear nothing but the
distant cries of seagulls
and the whipping wind.
A great calm settles
within me.
The sun sets over Beaufort's marsh.

Story Wiggins, 7th Grade
Beaufort Academy

Nancy Ricker Rhett

7

Childhood Memories

By Nancy Ricker Rhett

A Family Vacation on the Barrier Islands

In Beaufort, with its unique geography, a trip to the beach used to be an enormous undertaking. There is hardly any "mainland" in Beaufort County - it's all winding waterways, creeks, mile wide sounds, seemingly endless marshscapes, a few islands of major proportions, and, at the ocean's edge, aptly named strips called barrier islands. These are our beaches.

In the early days there were no bridges. The few main roads were usually oyster shell and dirt, and ferries transported everything across the rivers. The only reliable transportation was your own boat propelled by whatever wind and tide allowed, and your own sense of direction.

Nancy Ricker Rhett

Both my father and mother were born in Beaufort in 1900. It was their stories of camping at the beach that I remember most vividly.

My ancestors probably made the trip to the beach on a sailboat capable of carrying enough provisions for a long stay. Smaller boats ferried everything from the sailboat to shore where camp was established. With good weather, vacationers likely stayed several weeks.

My mother's side of the family built shacks at the beach with the flotsam or jetsam that drifted up and materials brought from town. These beach houses were expendable. Placed on a dune well above the high water mark to catch the sea breezes, no one expected them to last past the next hurricane. One-room creations, they always had a covered porch, sometimes a detached cookhouse and a boardwalk across the dunes to the water's edge. There was always a barrel on the roof to catch rainwater for drinking and bathing. Grandfather Elliott, Beaufort's only doctor, was a stickler for hygiene, and baths were a required regimen. "Rooms" inside were partitioned with brown paper, one side for the boys to sleep in and one side for the girls. Inevitably, someone got pushed through to the other side.

On my father's side, Grandpa Chandler was a sail, tent, and awning-maker in New York City. His textbook on awning design is still used as reference by awning makers today. He designed tents for Ringling Brothers and PT Barnum, but the best tent of all was the tent he designed for the Arabian sheik, because we had the prototype! We used it every summer.

The cook tent was located at the north end of the string with its flaps up. It was the center of activity. The sleeping tents were lined up along the beach, well away from the incoming tide and from foliage that harbored mosquitoes.

Shortly after World War II, when I was a child, we lugged long wooden ammunition crates to the beach to store food because the islands were inhabited by wild pigs and goats as well as 'coon and 'possums who raided our stores at night. We brought in all our drinking water, and fifty-pound blocks of ice from the old icehouse in Burton. The ice was wrapped in sawdust and burlap, then buried in the sand above the high tide line where it lasted two weeks, even in the August heat. It's amazing how cold the sand is only two feet down.

Camping on an outer island meant no communication with the rest of the world. There were no storm warnings, and what looked like a front moving through could have been far worse. Mother said that one squall was really the beginning of a hurricane and their only shelter was behind the dunes. They were beaten relentlessly by wind and rain and they lost their camp and all their possessions. They were lucky enough to salvage boats after the storm so that they could get home. Fortunately, it was only the fringe of the hurricane and not a direct hit. After the beach had been substantially eroded by storms, we camped in the middle of the island and had access to both inlets.

Henry - Henrietta

My Great-grandfather came to Beaufort from New Hampshire right after the Civil War to work with Mr. Waterhouse running a steam mill to gin cotton. The steam mill was on the Beaufort waterfront, where wagons and ships could easily load and unload cotton bales. It was discovered that steam mill/cotton gin was a prototype of Eli Whitney's invention — one of the first ever made.

In 1929, when the Great Depression struck, my father was let go from his job in Oklahoma and he and my mother and sister returned to Beaufort. They arrived with fifty cents to their name. Papa was grateful for whatever work he could find. He drove trucks, did carpentry, brick laying, and house painting. Mr. Henry Ford offered, through his manager, to purchase the gin and Papa, who needed money to support his family, agreed to sell it. It may now be seen in Henry Ford's Museum in Dearborn, Michigan.

Papa never met Mr. Ford, but well after completion of the business transaction there was a knock at the door. The stranger gave papa the keys to a shiny black car "*Compliments of Mr. Ford.*" To honor the occasion the family named the car *Henry*.

During WWII, we lived on a farm near Sheldon. Papa needed a truck more than he needed a car, so he cut the back end off of *Henry* and added a pick up bed in the rear. Newly adorned with a "bustle," *Henry* was re-christened "*Henrietta.*"

Henrietta needed a paint job and paint was scarce and expensive during the war. Since our house was large and housing was very limited, people in the area were asked to make room in their homes for pilots from the Naval Air Station and their families. We had two families living with us. We may have been crowded, but we all made the best of it. Sometimes, good things came from unexpected sources. Knowing Papa's need, the pilots surprised him one day with enough paint to redecorate *Henrietta.* Mr. Ford once said that his cars could be painted any color so long as it was black. The paint he was given was battleship gray. So, now we had a chopped off, bustle added, battleship gray pickup — a far cry from the shiny black car that Papa had started with almost fifteen years before. I have very fond memories of *Henrietta*. She was a wonderful place to play. You could make forts on the back, and slide down the fenders. The running boards were good spots for doll tea parties, and the hood folded up on each side so you could see all the parts inside. The windshield pushed out and was held in place by two brackets so you could feel the wind in your face as you went down the road. I remember being bundled in blankets with Mother and Papa on each side of me, lying on the bed of the truck to watch meteor showers in the night. It was cozy, dark, and magical. On occasion Papa would let me pull out the knob that said "Choke" on its shiny silver face. He said I was helping him make the car run better. I loved it. I also remember that the shaft of the choke was where he kept extra rubber bands.

Gradually *Henrietta* grew older and less used. When I was fourteen, two old men offered Papa three hundred dollars for *Henrietta*. Papa agonized. It was like selling a family member. But he knew them and they wanted to fix her up to use as their fishing car. Papa really didn't have time to fuss with her much anymore, so reluctantly, he sold her. I imagine that she rather liked the idea of being restored and useful again. I hated to see her go, but I'll always have warm memories of the four-wheeled member of our family.

Who would have dreamed Eli Whitney's cotton gin could turn into Mr. Ford's car?

Horns and Whistles

When I was a child, life in Beaufort revolved around horns and whistles. When I stayed at my Grandmother's little house on Port Republic Street, it was the whistle that scared the dickens out of me. Long before daylight, the loud, mournful sound of a steam whistle emanated from the Oyster Factory across the river, signaling that for many, the work-day had begun. It was a chilling sound to a child, and I could clearly picture some night monster bellowing ominously. I won't forget it.

Nor can I forget the noon whistle, actually a fire siren, that told the townspeople that twelve o'clock had arrived. One day my cousins and I heard the siren, and thought no more about it until it kept on wailing. Looking over towards town, for they lived on Lady's Island, we could see a tower of smoke. Their father came home to tell us that the dime store on Bay Street was on fire. Our hearts were broken. More than just the store went up in smoke that day.

The Magic Tree

Beaufort has many wonderful trees, long-limbed live oaks that have even been given names, like the one on the bluff overlooking the river that's known as "Moonlight on the Bay." But I must confess that I had the grandest of them all. In our back yard in the triangle formed by the roads at Gardens Corner, there was an avenue of eight magnificent oak trees, some of which still stand. They lined the road that, from Revolutionary days, came from Beaufort and formed a "T" at what is now Rt. 17. At that time it was known as the "King's Highway," down which Washington traveled in 1792. Because Benjamin Garden (cousin to Alexander Garden who had developed the flower, "Gardenia") had had a trading post there where the roads met, it became known as Gardens Corner.

Long ago, on cold winter days when people were waiting for transportation, they would light a fire up against a tree trunk so that the heat would be reflected back for ultimate warmth, One tree must have been ideal for this, because it had charred and burned over the years until there was a hole completely through the massive trunk, leaving a doorway on each side and a "ceiling" about seven feet up. Grownups had to duck a bit to enter, but the door was just the right height for children. Branching off about ten feet up was the "chimney," the remains of a large angled branch that had broken off. You could see the sky through it, but rain didn't come in because it jutted out at just the proper angle. Inside the tree, about four feet across and three feet wide was my room. There was even a charred shelf in there just the right height to store tiny teapot and cups.   The floor was always dry and sandy, and even though the walls were charred, the ancient black soot didn't rub off. For playmates and certain invited grownups whom I deemed would appreciate the magic of being inside a living, massive tree, this was indeed a magic place, a perfect hideaway for a child's tea parties.

Gardens Corner

My Father built Gardens Corner Motel and Restaurant, a place known up and down the East Coast as a Quality Court with the restaurant recommended by Gourmet. It was a fascinating life, and as my Mother would say, the world came to us. I met so many diverse and even famous people who stayed there, it was like having a party every night. One such night I remember we had John Donne (the poet's descendant), Mr. Ballentine (as in the ale), and Mr. Fargo (as in Wells) all seated at our dinner table. Guests would return year after year. There were famous writers like .Rachel Carson and John Marquand, musicians and entertainers like Keely Smith and Louis Prima, (They used to entertain at Parris Island, and she would let me help choose her evening dress for the performance!) and famous polo players ftom all over the world.

Looking back the guests who most influenced me were the artists: Dick Bishop, Boris Artzybasheff, John Day, and, most memorable, Preston Blair. He was a Disney illustrator, a delightful man who would sit down and sketch Mickey, Donald,and Bugs. He had just finished work on "Fantasia", and he gave some sketches to me.

Since my Father sang and played the banjo, inevitably people who were musical returned to our house where the piano was, and the party would continue way past my bedtime. Even though we were far from "civilization", the world did indeed come to us.

Parties, Parties, Parties

Since Beaufort was at the "end of the world", with only one way in by land, it could have been a very boring place. But there has always been a tradition of partying here from early plantation days. People traveled by boat to toast any occasion, often staying for several days. During WWI, it was a treat to ferry over to Parris Island for an Officers' Ball. Parties became the reward for life during hard times. Conviviality didn't suffer. Not ones to break tradition, when World War II demanded rationing of goods, my parents started giving what became known as "Pint and Pound" parties. And these became weekly. Guests brought a pint of what their ration stamps would allow and a pound of whatever meat they could afford. Oysters were roasted, shrimp were piled high on platters, and the delicacies from the creek in front of our house would be served. Music and song mingled in the air with wonderful aromas and light-hearted laughter. These parties became year-round, even in the coldest winter months and on the hottest summer nights. Nowadays, oyster roasts and songfests are becoming a novelty, a nostalgic glimpse of the way Beaufort once was.

South Carolina

South Carolina borders the ocean
Our ocean has sea turtles,
Jelly fish, sharks, shrimps,
Octopuses, alligators and sting rays.
South Carolina always has African Gullah Festival.
Sometimes we have hurricanes.

Reginald Washington, 5th Grade
James J. Davis Elementary

Michael Housemans, 3rd Grade - M.C. Riley Elementary

Law Enforcement Complex

Beaufort has the LEC where the jail is. People have been pulled over for speeding. Police are good at that I like police. In SC police caught 200 people. Is that a lot? I think that is too much. My Dad is a deputy sheriff. My Dad's friends help him pull people who are speeding over. He was in a drug-bust. He caught 2 people. One of his friends helped him. I was with him when we went to the LEC.

Kyle Blankenship, 2nd Grade - Shell Point Elementary

Jermaine Wright, 5th Grade - St. Helena's Elementary

15

SHORE IV: *Elisions*

Homing, in my newest
innocence, to the sea
as a vexed child come
at twilight to sit by its
parent, keen for wisdom,

I uncry to the Night
Heron's call each cry-
back, at the shadows
through which it wings,
of my wayward stanzas,

raze the metaphors where
risen and receding tide
whisper as they brush
in passing: shores wait
upon the moon's whims,

waive every last wave-
combed iamb, current-
anxious rhythm or wind
railed at to spell it
again — louder, slower,

and muting all verses
in my throat to prayer,
listen at this late hour
as might salt listen
to the dissolving rains.

Charles H. Ash

Barbara LaPlante

16

Finger snapping trout... 
and open-mouthed bass
swaying in
a stiff current
still.
Still and silent yet
ruffling clouds of
chocolate truffle
mud
pluff black.
Rippling rings
patterned across
the sky's reflection
and dripping sounds of liquid libations
into innocent canals.
This silence is deafening.

Scott Gordon

Penny Russell

17

Lana Hefner - "Coastal Lights"

Ease's Chapel

A boilin-off indigo sort of a March night, muzzy cloud
smoke-thick; out in the blackness, blacker forms
loomin there: somethin round, reckon a pillar, walls
like they was dead, buried and been got at by worms.

Bag of long staple cloud snag a horn of the moon,
rip, go to spillin stars, ooh!, all out cross night,
til ain't long, honey, fore it pourin down stars,
blackness packin in a congregation of starlight.

Starlight! Starlight! Mercy, this ol holey, empty
holy blackness jam full up with jumpy shadow;
bricks awaverin the way water sometime ripple
its shadow upside a willow. Moon for a window,

slabs of streaky-shinin sky for roofbeam, door hung
to a mist comin on midnight for mornin like a wonder.
Had me some wine, a couple crust, I bow my head, then
raise up, sing Hallelujah at that blackness yonder.

Charles H. Ash

Sea Island Scape

Sea island scape painting a densely filled
    field of vision green.

Dizzying depth and impenetrable forests
    hide life teeming forth.

Woven canopies groping for the light to feed
    gently gnarled roots for hundreds of years,

This tree will not topple easy.

Scott Gordon

A Tree

There is a tree by my house
It is so B-I-G
One tree that's in the
South Carolina State is Palmetto.

Now there's another tree
That I like
It's not ugly or beautiful
It's just right.
It's an oak

Pepcie Anthly, 5th Grade
James J. Davis Elementary

Lynn McLaren

Rope

Ratty old tattered
    snake coiled
    in a pile
    on a boat's chine
    soft.
This simplest of tools
    connected close
    to the harvest
    of a fresh hemp field
    potent.
This simplest of technologies
    sung electric
    by George Washington
himself
Grow it and they will come,
one by one.
From the ground by hand,
    carefully woven into
    its perfect form
    by hand,
    carried to the dock. . .
by hand.
It is the hand that suffers the most
    when, grasping the

threadbarren serpent,
    a force of twenty knots
cuts to the bone.
It is the hand suffering from
    lockjaw and
    lactic acid
    that refuses to let go
    clenching stiff and stern
    yet pulling off a
two-finger pirouette
    on moment's notice.
    It is the hand clutching this
    pencil, remembering the pain,
    and telling legends
cut deep
    in the lines and the cracks
    from the wrist to the fingers.
It is the hand taming the wild coils
soaked in salt.
It is the hands raised above one's
head shielding the joyous glare of a
day's end
hard.

Scott Gordon

Will Cook

Oyster Boats In Summer...

were never meant to be.
Upside down in knee-high grass,
waiting for the gray season
of salt grit and croaker sacks.
For strong black men in hip boots
dipping oars through the crack-of-dawn fog,
soft in the sweet Gullah rhythms of their morning.
No color but flannel shirts.
Clusters chinked across the deck.
Solid.

But not in August
when caked mud sifts away,
fine powder for dirt dobbers
nesting in the hull shade.
Wooden tombstones waiting to be turned,
Dragged back down the bank
And launched,
And lapped at.

Ellen Malphrus

Eric Horan

Dockdaze

By Melba Cooper

Mylar sheeting unrolled from bank to bank, bridge to town, fresh pulled aluminum reflections. Dolphins broke the surface blowing away the illusion. From the ocean and up the ICW the Beaufort River mirrored the July sunset.

Thunderstorm threats had quieted the afternoon wind, transforming the river into a flow of thick smooth mercury — a rising thermometer that cooled the hot air. The light above reflected in a molten surface, white silver, bluish gray, orange — flashed deep on the surface. I sat cross-legged close to the edge of the dock. The platform hung 10 feet above the water level. I leaned over to see bits of marsh detritus floating by, reassuring myself that what I saw was just river water. To my left the McTeer Bridge arched from Meridian Rd. to the Port Royal Marina. My eye followed the east end of the steel rainbow to the western settlement of condos, boats, vertical masts. From Stewbee's Bar, Irene's mellow guitar music strummed across the river. Lime green bands of Lowcountry spartina stretched to my right, filtering the river's flow through the Cut.

The colors that attracted me to the river were above the marsh line. Dark thick thunderheads amassed in the south. Brilliant yellows and oranges to the west. Clouds, fibrous masses of combed cotton, dyed in indigo moisture, the blue of dark jeans, faded cut-offs, light summer shirts, layered northward in a zigzag configuration of thinning tufts — gray-blue clouds stretched across cumulus oranges caught the explosions of yellow wind drafts in the upper atmosphere.

Filled with the ever-changing beauty of the moment, I was here alone. How many times I had come to the river alone to sit and dream, pray, celebrate, reflect, cry. Sometimes the call of the river was too strong. Its calm too inviting.

Again searching for a metaphor, "was it really a Mylar balloon surface?" the river looked softly crinkled. I struggled for descriptive words. Maybe. A dolphin broke the water in an easy rhythm. Another joined. I smiled. They played south against the tide, looking for incoming mullet? A southern breeze touched my cheek, then puffed stronger. I looked to the darkening southern sky, smelling rain. Heat flashes. Warm waters of emotion rose to my throat, to my eyes. The tearducts seemed too small to be an outlet for so much. My skin was just a container for rising blood and water, filled to overflowing, my stomach ballooned. I shook and felt the sunset's grief.

A crescent moon appeared way down river. Thin reptile skins of air textured the river's slick surface. Parabolic wind shapes spread upriver. The air smelled wet. The parabolas joined each other forming curved irregular patterns. Ancient weather skins stretched over the shiny surface, encasing small mirrored pools of orange light. The wind increased, the first drops of sprinkle mixed with the unwiped tears on my face. I turned my back to the river and looked up at the bike propped above me. Towers of salmon clouds rose above the distant woods. I brushed away the water and pushed up on the dock. I felt heavy and reluctant to go home and yet needful. The mountain slick tires gently cushioned the ride across the dock's weathered boards and onto the asphalt mile leading home. I'd been alone long enough for today.

Kevin Thompson, 10th Grade - Hilton Head High School

25

Beaufort Waterfront Park At Sunrise

Tabby stanchions, like sentinels, stand at dawn to greet the rising sun,
While the ghostly shadow of the moon recedes in the distant sky.

The tides go in — the tides go out in never ending rhythm.

While the rising orb in glowing orange reflects in the water below,
A salty scent is in the air — the mist begins to clear.
As the fiery sun extends its rays up from the vast horizon,
It heralds the start of another day, the promise of a blessing —
So crops can grow to light the world with awe-inspiring splendor.

The clock of the centuries ticks along in many epochs of time.
Ages of man have come and gone, but the sun is always there.

Walter Dennis

Lana Hefner - "September Sky"

Bluffton's
Brighton Beach and All Joy

An abbreviated history by Carolyn C. Smith

righton Beach, better known by the locals as All Joy, was part of an original Kings' grant to the Lords Proprietor. The property was inherited by Mr. C.E. Ulmer who formed a partnership with Mr. Thomas O. Lawton to develop 100 acres along the Maye River. When they failed to agree on a selling price for the parcels, Mr Lawton purchased the 100 acres from Mr. Ulmer in 1918.

In 1926 the land was surveyed and divided into lots and Mr. Lawton who had lived in Garnet, SC, on Brighton Plantation, named the property "Brighton Beach" At first the lots sold for $50.00 each. By the 1940s they were $250.00 apiece and today you can expect to pay about $200,000.00 for a waterfront lot.

Mr. Lawton sold all of his lots personally using handwritten deeds, a bond for title, and permitting buyers to pay as they could. Fifteen acres on the Maye River was set aside for the Lawton Family and is still owned by Mr. Lawton's heirs.

A public strip, known as All Joy Beach, was provided for all property owners to enjoy the river, and one acre was donated to Beaufort County for a public boat ramp.

Antoinette and Harry Walton All purchased land along the river from Mr. Lawton and built the All Joy Hotel next to the public boat ramp. The Hotel burned in the 1930s, but locals continue to refer to the area as All Joy Beach and the All heirs continue to reside in the vicinity.

The small dirt lanes laid out during the original survey bear the names of local flavor such as oyster, mullet, trout and flounder. The inner roads were originally given numbers (except for #7, which Mr. Lawton did not like). With the advent of the 911 emergency system, the numbering system had to be changed, and at the suggestion of Martha Crapse, the streets were renamed to honor the home-towns of some of the summer residents. They now bear such names as Scotia, Lura, Allendale, or Brunson. The main road to Bluffton is called All Joy Road.

Oyster Street has always been my favorite place. My parents, Walter and Martha Crapse, made it their home in the 1940s, and I was born and raised there. Life was fun on Oyster Street, even though in the 1950s there were only about a dozen permanent families living in the Brighton Beach area. Life was much more exciting in the summer months with seasonal residents remaining until after Labor Day. Time was devoted to fishing, crabbing, swimming and water-skiing on the river and of course spending hours on the sand bar. We returned home sunburned, water-logged, tired, hungry and the happiest a human being could be.

Lynda Potter - "Tall Chimney"

The Summer Palace

By Carolyn Bremer

It was always to their credit that they spoke to us, is what we said in later years about our neighbors at the Estill Beach Colony. When the two-family entourage of four adults, nine children, two dogs, a cat and five kittens arrived at a rental home on the May River in July of 1966, life at the little enclave was surely never the same again.

It was our first ever occasion to sleep over on the banks of a saltwater river and each day of our allotted two-week holiday was a treat.

One of the ladies of the Colony sat every afternoon in her chair and nodded and gazed at our antics. Another neighbor lent us his treasured dock space to park our 14' wooden bateau; the one that carried our group in two loads to the Sand Bar and hauled skiers through the river on huge old orange wooden skis ... skis so long and so wide that a person could lie down on them. The year was 1966 and all was right in our world.

Computer enhanced photograph by Carolyn Bremer

In the Savannah Sunday paper next spring, after months of reading want ads, we found, "For Sale, Estill Beach SC. Summer cottage on May River. Dock included." A quick phone call confirmed an appointment. It was a cold day, dank and damp. The house was concrete block inside and outside and the furnishings were minimal, but we bought it within hours.

We walked through the little cottage like it was fit for kings and we were the royalty. Hence the "Summer Palace" was born, and lived in and loved for eighteen years.

As time went on we realized that the fireplace that folks came from miles to sit in front of didn't even keep a small blaze going. And the only shower, in the only bathroom, flowed only in tiny plops of water. And we learned that three on a flush was not too bad.

For the first five years, the *Summer Palace* sported no telephone and no television. Our families had the numbers of the three neighbors who enjoyed communication with the outside world when calls were necessary. We never missed either convenience. The children hiked and biked on the shores, swam, skied, fished in and studied the waters of the mighty May. Sundays were cherished days, for storekeeper Morris Rabinowich (The Planter's Mercantile) went to Gottlieb's Bakery in Savannah at the crack of dawn to pick up trays of delicious sweet rolls and good breads for everyone to enjoy.

Bluffton in the late '60s and '70s was not only a state of mind, it was a place in time. Today, the neighborhood has grown in magnitude and beauty. Gone are the days when one could call from porch to porch, all the cottages are enclosed with the air-conditioning set on 'high'. We sold the Summer Palace and it was torn down to make room for a 3-story island-style home with a view of the river. Our new home on Myrtle Island is replete with the amenities of life. The gentle passage of time has been replaced with a hurry-burly life. Somehow, we never feel the togetherness of family as much here as we did there! A little nostalgia for the old times creeps in now and then. But, blessed are the Bremers and forever happy the good Lord took us and placed us down in our heartland to live a portion of life.

Patrick Milhouse, 4th Grade
Michael C. Riley Elementary

Cecelia Barraro, 4th Grade
Michael C. Riley Elementary

Times Have Changed, But The Beloved Sandbar Remains Pretty Much The Same.

By Annelore Harrell

It is almost the last Sandbar Sunday. George William is over at Walton Harper's playing chess. The grandchildren are all somewhere else. As comfortable as it is, it is almost the last Sandbar Sunday of the season. I put on my bathing suit, pull on a pair of shorts, add a long-sleeved shirt and head out the door.

It doesn't take very long to ride around the end of Myrtle Island to the sandbar if you have a boat with a motor. But, let me tell you, it's a long way around if you are pullin' oars on a big ol' wooden bateau against the tide. We did that more than a few times, when we wanted to go crabbing in the nearby creeks.

But today we are in a nice boat that goes smooth and fast. There are people from one end of the almost mile-long sandbar to the other. Boats of all sizes anchored so close you could almost jump from one to another.

Victoria Butler, 4th Grade - M.C. Riley Elementary

Bluffton old-timers are at this end, and newcomers at the end the tide covers first. There are all ages, all shapes, and all stages of sobriety. You visit with some on the beach and you wade out to chat with those on a party boat. Over across the sandbar, children are covered in black mud as they go boggin' on the creek side. An optimist is throwing a shrimp net. Dogs chase all over. Someone has beached a catamaran and is scrubbing down the hull. For the first time I hear Spanish spoken as I pass along. Out on the river, jet skis dodge kayaks and children ride a big inner tube behind a speedboat.

Cool chest and lawn chairs. Charcoal burners and beach umbrellas. Baby strollers and Frisbees. People everywhere, everywhere.

Last week when I had lunch with some of my oldest and dearest friends from way back, they reminded me of the times they had been to Bluffton over 50 years ago.

"Remember when we went to the sandbar?" Carol Ruth said. "There were six of us and we went over in your bateau with that little 3 horse-power motor, and we decided to go skinny dippin'. There wasn't a soul around. If anybody was going to come by we could hear their motor long before they got close enough to see us. It was so still. Even if they were rowing we could hear. Well, we did. Go skinny dippin' that is. It was great fun. But we all got sunburned in places that, well, in those places. When we got back, showered and dressed, we were smeared full of Noxzema and couldn't bear to wear tight clothes.

"After supper we went down to The Fiddler at All Joy Beach. They had a jukebox but you couldn't dance 'cause they didn't have a license for that. We just had a Coke and listened to the music and heard somebody across the room talking about some girls who had been skinny-dippin on the sandbar that day. No one knew who they were, but so and so had some binoculars and had seen them out there. Well we never found out who so and so was, but we sure didn't jump up and say 'It was us out there today'."

Walking down the sandbar in 1999 is as different from that time as it could be, and yet the sandbar itself hasn't really changed much. It may have moved a bit here and added a bit more sand there... Do you think there might be a message there someplace?

Victoria Butler, 4th Grade - M.C. Riley Elementary

Caryl Sweet

Sandcastling

By Melba Cooper

Today I prowl the beach of Hunting Island, my snapshot sketchpad swinging from my neck. I snap some photos of a sandformation, roots, a turtle nesting area. But my real search today is for sandcastles. Children's sandcastles. I walk a mile down to South Beach and spot a group of children constructing a grid of moats — a mound of sand rising in the center. Four children are intent on their work of the day. I introduce myself and ask them about their castle. Ten-year- old Chris is the master planner. He explains the division of labor between himself, his eight-year-old brother, twelve-year-old sister, and the six year old "water-boy."

I look over the emerging design, noting the smooth shaped mound punctuated by shells. Ten of them formed the perimeter of a large egg-shaped oval, the outer protective walls of their castle fortress. Central to the design is a large mound with a yawning mouth guarded by teeth-shell fragments and a drawbridge into the interior fortress. A tall tower set atop the mound can be seen 25 yards down the beach marking the castle's location. Formed with dribbled wet sand, its peak ends in a fine point. In an innocent expression of pride, the children crouch to have their picture taken.

I snap several angles and sit down to listen. The master builder explains that he built the chapel as the first building. The nuns' quarters are in the mounded shapes that are equally spaced as bulwarks for the walls. The cemetery sports sprigs of marsh grass honoring the tombstone. Chris takes a stick and draws out the central living quarters.

We speak of symbols, of painting, of art and adventure. We speak of sandcastling in a fragile environment. They understand. They are the artists.

The children invited me back that afternoon to see their finished castle. I was delayed with adult responsibilities. When I returned they ran to me across the beach. I was too late, they shouted. The castle had been washed away. "It happened so fast!"

Amber Morgan, 2nd Grade - James J. Davis Elementary

Farming in Beaufort

By Graham Sanders 8th Grade

Beaufort's rich soil, accessibility to water, and warm climate make it an ideal farming region. Farming has been the backbone of America since it was settled in the early 1600's. Beaufort farmers grow fruits, tomatoes, peppers, onions, corn, wheat, sod, beans, and many more vegetables. While many farmers use new high-tech tractors and irrigation pumps, other farmers still employ the old methods such as ditches and plows.

Many different techniques are used to ensure a stable, successful crop. Most farmers chose to begin with a seedling plant rather than seeds because it provides a better assurance of survival. Farmers often put plastic down over the soils so that the plant does not lose the soil its roots are holding when the high winds and rains come. Another method of protecting the plants is to plant rye grass in rows between the plants before they are even put in the ground. This allows the grass to have enough time to grow so that it will protect the plants. Once the plant takes root, it can enjoy a successful growth in the rich soil and warm climate of Beaufort.

Nancy Easter White

Beaufort

Art Gore

Beaufort, South Carolina, is nestled between two historical cities: Savannah, Georgia, and Charleston, South Carolina, both of which are popular tourist attractions: however, Beaufort has a beauty and attraction of its own which lure thousands of visitors each year.

Old Sheldon Church was built in the 1700's. During the Revolutionary War and the Civil War, it was burned down. All that is standing today are several brick columns, but it is still one of the most popular sites in Beaufort, The church has an old water pump that still works, a graveyard, and several tombs. One of the most interesting points about Old Sheldon Church is its location. The trees next to the winding country road have grown like a canopy covering the area. It feels like a tunnel as one drives through it.

Many other historical sites are found in Beaufort. Downtown Beaufort has a multitude of shops and restaurants, which are located along the waterfront. Tourists and residents can shop, eat, and walk along the sea wall. They may elect to enjoy a carriage ride in which a trained guide tells them the history and legends of the area.

The historical homes of Beaufort are beautiful. They often have large double porches and wide lawns. Some of the historical homes have been turned into popular bed and breakfasts like the Rhett and Beaufort Inns. Beaufort is a quaint town, whose smallness and intriguing past have made it a popular tourist attraction and an ideal location in which to live.

Maggie Cann, 8th Grade
Beaufort Academy

Carla Wynn 11th Grade - Beaufort High School

Beaufort is a beautiful county. One of the nicest places is the beach. At the beach you can swim and sometimes you can see dolphins. At the beach you can camp too! When you camp, you can see deer and reptiles. You also can take nature walks. "If you want to take walks you better wear shoes." There is a lighthouse there. It is a long way up, but worth it. If you were a journalist you would have a good bit to write about. Well I know one thing I don't want to leave Beaufort.

Sean Roos 4th Grade
Mossy Oaks Elementary

Marsh

The sun rises
Rises above the trees
It starts as small hints of yellow and red.
This in a vast blue sky
As it rises and rises
It seems as though the whole world awakens
Birds begin to sing and deer begin to feed
The marsh that was once just shadows
Is now a story of its own existence.

Ryan Bellamy, 11th Grade
Beaufort Academy

Coosaw Community Center

I like to imagine—to think of this spot—
What it was like a couple hundred years ago.
Yes, even further back to a time when this road
Was a trail to other villages and settlements;
When the Ogeechee and Coosaw Indians were here.

History tells us that
The Blacks and Whites were here.
That this very site was used for prayer meetings;
For giving their supplications to God.

I hearsay that there were orange trees flourishing.
A schoolhouse was created by families
To pass on knowledge to their children.

Folks had farms; cows, goats, pigs, turkeys, chickens.

Many families remained
And lived out their lives, here, on Coosaw.

This corner was just far enough from Lucy Creek
And its treacherous waters to stop and rest;
To meet family, exchange greetings,
News of Beaufort Town-
News of births, deaths, losses and gains.

Perhaps the young exchanged their
First love-glances here;
Planned their future and families.
This very soil holds the grains of sand
Upon which their feet trod.

I can feel their presence;
Almost hear their calls.

Under these great oaks
Must have stood
Rejoicing men and women
After the "Big Shoot."

Freedom!

Coming on down through the decades,
The young became old,
Took their exits,
And were laid down to rest.

Their children came and gathered here-
As was the custom—
And so are we here today,
To honor and dedicate to the future—

Wilhelmina Mitchell

Rebecca Davenport - "Red Painting" 1997

The Teacherage

Beaufort has watched me and others turn into octogenarians in the past forty-five years.

We have watched the sleepy little seaside town turn into a fast growing metropolis with a cosmopolitan population.

Ah! The Beaufort Gazette only came once a week, and most everybody knew everybody. If you ate out, you ate at Harry's. Most every house had its own cook.

I was house mother at the Teacherage the last years it was needed for the young women that were hired by the Beaufort County School Board. I had a cook and housekeeper to help me care for fourteen teachers. There were no motels, no hotel or tourist home. Young women were still chaperoned.

The old Teacherage is now a bed and breakfast place called Two Suns - $75 per B&B, and the teachers were to pay $12 each week. Times have changed.

–Hildred Fern Collier

Barbara Shipman - "Tidalholm "

PENN CENTER:
National Historic Landmark

By Nancy Gebhardt

Some ideas are tough as well as inspired and can survive the passage of time. Penn Center on St. Helena Island is living proof. For well over a century this beloved institution has faithfully served the local community, educating its citizens and preserving their history, culture and environment. Founded in 1862 by Philadelphia missionaries Laura Towne and Ellen Murray, the Penn School set out to teach "self sufficiency" to the former slaves of St. Helena's plantations during the period of transition to freedom. Charlotte Forten, an African-American teacher also from the City of Brotherly Love, joined the two founders. Even as the Civil War raged throughout the region, some eighty students in the fall of 1862 were learning how to read and write and how to take care of their families and their farms. And now, one hundred and thirty-five years later, Penn Center Inc. is the repository of Sea Island Gullah history and is visited by citizens and scholars from all over the world.

Six miles east of Beaufort, S.C. on Highway 21 and a right turn onto Martin Luther King Drive brings you within minutes to the Penn Center. Since 1974, when Penn School's 50-acre campus was designated a National Historic Landmark District, restoration has been ongoing. The restoration project and raising money to support it are top priorities for Emory Campbell, its Director.

Mr. Campbell takes special pride in Penn's land use program, particularly the "Sea Island Preservation Project." Community leaders from as far away as Florida and North Carolina attend six months of weekend training sessions in leadership, environmental policy, legal aid for landowners, sustainable economic development and community coalition building.

Penn Center sponsors the PACE Program (Program for Academic and Cultural Enrichment) providing students, ages 6-13, tutoring and homework assistance in an atmosphere that encourages critical thinking and problem solving, and in partnership with the University of South Carolina, it sponsors a highly effective Early Childhood/At Risk Families initiative.

The York W. Bailey Cultural Museum, named for a Penn graduate who returned to St. Helena to practice medicine, houses a renowned collection of historical materials on African Americans of the sea islands. Unique artifacts, photographs, books, personal papers, video and audiotapes are available to researchers as well as amateur historians.

> *"My elder sister and some cousins from Hilton Head Island attended Penn School, and of course everyone packed a big trunk. Then they took a boat to Savannah and from there a bus to St. Helena. It was an all day trip... We didn't see them again until Christmas! Then everyone noticed how they'd 'got culture' over there. They spoke English! We spoke only Gullah, you know at home, but they came back speaking English. And they had polite manners and they had learned some fine skills. Oh, they were greatly admired. We all thought Penn was a special place.... and still is. "* Emory Campbell

The event leading to the founding of the original Penn School was known as "the day of the gun-shoot at Bay Point." On November 7, 1861 the Federal fleet successfully assaulted Forts Beauregard and Walker and seized control of Port Royal Sound. From that day former slaves left behind on the sea island plantations were free in fact, but not yet free by law. For want of better terminology, the island blacks were called "contrabands" of war. The Federal Government, suddenly confronted with a moral and legal dilemma of immense proportions, saw a solution in economics. The profits from cotton crops deserted by plantation owners were a potential boon for the Union war effort. Former island slaves knew cotton culture better than anyone and were enlisted by the government to harvest and re-plant the lucrative crop. This economic venture was seen as an opportunity to prepare black workers for self-sufficiency. The "Port Royal Experiment," as it was called, became a guided transition from slavery to freedom. Missionaries and teachers from the North flocked to the Lowcountry to help with the project. Thus reconstruction was underway for the isolated sea island populations before the Emancipation Proclamation and well before the end of the Civil War.

Will Pitt, while attending
Lady's Island Middle School

Laura Towne, a Unitarian from Philadelphia, with g
positive thinking and practical hard-headedness, was
aide on St. Helena Island. She arrived on April 15, 1
beauty and the people of the place where she would
spend the rest of her life. In one of her first letters
home she expresses the awe she felt in her new sur-
roundings. *"I wish I could sketch. the trees (which)
are so picturesque. I have seen white herons . . . there
is the skin of an alligator Lying in the yard. I never
in my life saw such garden roses."* Her diary, one of
the best records of the Port Royal Experiment,

describes the confusion of a fledgling bureaucracy and the war-time desperation of the people it was intended to serve. *"We go again tomorrow upon a visit to the poor anxious people who have lived on promises (of pay) and are starving for clothes and food."*

Soon Laura Towne and Ellen Murray, her Quaker friend, who also dedicated her life to the project on St. Helena, discovered their mission. It was education, the key to an improved quality of life for the people they came to help. They opened the first Penn School in their living room at the Oaks Plantation for nine adults. Within a month they had enrolled over eighty students and moved to the old Brick Church. The following year their pre-fabricated three-room schoolhouse arrived by boat, sent by the Philadelphia Freedmen's Association.

The black students on St. Helena's Island entered freedom with a thirst for education. The missionary ladies stressed practical and home arts but also included academic subjects in the curriculum, with great emphasis on reading, history, arithmetic and penmanship. Penn School students may have learned much more – ingenuity, self-reliance, and service to the community – from the examples set by their teachers. And although the influence of Penn School on its students was significant, Laura Towne saw that influence reaching only a limited number of families. Toward the end of her life she sought out Hollis Burke Frissell of the Hampton Institute, hoping he would take up her cause.

Frissell was reputed to be the country's leading authority on education for blacks. He was enthusiastic about continuing the work begun by Laura Towne and was eager to propose an industrial education program for Penn School. The isolation of St. Helena Island accounted for the preservation of the population's Gullah language and culture. Also, Frissell thought, the Islanders were uniquely self sufficient and successful with land ownership. St. Helena presented an opportunity to test progressive ideas both in agricultural practices and education. Penn Normal and Industrial and Agricultural School, sponsored by the Hampton Institute, was incorporated at the turn of the century. A board of trustees who were highly educated, well-to-do, socially conscious citizens, and mostly Northerners ran it.

The first Superintendent of Industries at the new Penn School was Hampton graduate P.W. Dawkins. He organized "farmers' conferences" modeled after one initiated by Booker T. Washington at Tuskegee. St. Helena farmers drew up a constitution that embodied their basic ideas and principles: to raise their own food supply, to stay out of debt, to encourage a high standard of social behavior, to improve the community's schools and churches and to acquire property. Later, well-loved Superintendent Joshua Blanton established the annual "Farmers' Fair" which was revived in 1980 as Penn Center's celebration of traditions called "Heritage Days."

Diane Britton Dunham

Rossa Cooley and Grace House replaced Penn's founders in the early 1900's. The two charming and energetic young ladies caused heads to turn as they rode horseback around the island to observe living and working conditions. Their aim was to "bring island life into the classroom" and to prepare students for the life they would lead. Community service was ingrained. Student volunteers converted the old school house into a residence for an elder citizen known as "Aunt Jane." One European visitor wrote: "I have never seen better public spirit."

In the 1920's Penn won recognition as a model community and center for progressive ideas. Miss Cooley's dream of an "All Year School" blended academic learning and practical skills. Government sponsored farm and home demonstrations brought innovation, modern techniques and international visitors. Penn entered and won many prizes in the Better Homes in America Campaign. Their first winning demonstration was Jessamine cottage, a teacher's home, which still stands on the campus.

Eventually the "All Year School" was closed and in 1948 it became Penn Community Services, Inc, a development program with a day care center, health clinic, youth recreation program and midwives institute that also provided funding for college scholarships and farm loans.

Shalonda Bryan - 11th Grade, Beaufort High School

In 1961 Marion Wright led the Board of Trustees in an endorsement of the civil rights revolution in South Carolina and Penn Center became the only place in the South where blacks and whites could meet. During the 1960's Penn hosted many meetings and conferences of the Southern Christian Leadership Conference. Martin Luther King Jr. was a frequent visitor.

This durable institution has been in continuous service since 1862 and has played a role in two defining points in the course of American history. Freed slaves were first educated at the Penn School, ...And a hundred years later, blacks and whites got together at Penn Center to launch the civil rights movement.

Penn School's founder, Laura Towne, wrote in a letter home, *The things going on here (at Penn) ought not to be forgotten nor lost.*

Will Cook

PACE Youth Counselors

Contributed by the PACE Program of the Penn Center

In 1995, "youth counselors" for the PACE Program took a three-week course in writing. They were asked to write honestly and truthfully about themselves and to say whatever was in their hearts. The following paragraphs are excerpted from the journals of the the PACE "Youth Counselor."

"I come from a family of farm workers. My ancestors all used to work on the farm. Some did it for slave work others did it for money. My mother started working on the farm when she was real young. She worked with her stepmother too. My great-great-grand mother worked for slavery when she was alive. When my brother was young he used to work on the farm with my mother. I never worked on the farm. I just help out with the garden at home. My mom, my grandma, and my great grandma like to grow gardens. Mostly my family is made up of farm workers. Sometimes I dream about being a teacher. I am good with bad children but I like good children the most. I like to go to school too. I never dreamed about my future before. But I know that's what I want to be." - *Tyesha Jenkins -age 13*

Will Cook

"I come from a big family. I have 6 brothers and 2 sisters. I care about my family and I know they care about me. My brothers spoil me until its a crying shame. They always give me three things: 1 love 2. money 3. places to sleep. My aunts and uncles are all over the world. Some in New York, Washington, Augusta, South Carolina. Every time they see me they always say things that make me feel good. My father told me that we had famous singers and actresses inside my family. Well, that's my big family.

The hardest thing about being me is being short and skinny. People give me names like Shorty and Lil' Bit and they say "You so skinny you can fit through a Cheerio!" Also my voice is very squeaky sometimes. My teacher would call me Squeaky Rogers and the class would laugh. My voice is so squeaky and still is. I guess the hardest thing about being me is my voice! The best thing about being me is liking jewelry. My mother told me when I was growing up that she used to want a daughter whose hands were filled up with rings, all 10 fingers, and bracelets all the way up her arm and earrings too I told my mom maybe one day I will wear those things. Sometimes I dream about being a teacher. I made the honor roll in the 5th grade and every time you make the honor roll you get a chance to be a teacher and you get to join this club called "Teachers Of Tomorrow". I love to work with little kids." *Nikitress Rogers Age 15*

"I come from a family of hard working black brothers and sisters, working together. They all once worked on a big farm back in the woods of my grandmother's house. They didn't enjoy coming from school and having to work on a farm 'till the end of day. The other part of my family was the "clean" family. They mostly stayed in the house and kept it clean. All the children had to keep the animals healthy and well while the mother went out to work since there wasn't a father. Through it all both sides of the family, they survived. The hardest thing about me is I'm so tall. When I was young it didn't bother me because everyone was my height but now I'm taller than most people.

Will Cook

But it doesn't bother me when they tease me because I think I'm pretty on the outside even though I'm tall. I think if you think you are pretty, then you are. I just can't figure out why God does all these many things for us when we can't see him to give him anything back." *Shalonda Pope - age 14*

"I come from a family of people who like to work. My mom is a really hard worker. She drives a tractor -trailer truck. No one thought that mom could handle a big truck besides our family. My dad is also, a hard worker he's an electrician who is serious about his work. My grandmother is a nurse and she takes her work very serious. She makes sure that we are healthy. My grandfather is a contractor I know he is serious with his work. My brother is not really a hard worker, he goofs off a lot. I come from a family of people who like to work. The hardest thing about being me is being skinny. I'm always being teased and called toothpick. Every time I hear that name I get a little angry but not a lot. The best thing about being me is, being able to move quick and fast."
Hassan Johnson age 13

Lisa Chamberlain, while attending Beaufort High School

Will Cook

Melba Cooper - "Miss Annie's House"

Sea Island Quilters

By Anne Louttit

I moved to Beaufort in May, 1991 and not two weeks went by before I was invited by a dear neighbor to attend a Sea Island Quilter's Meeting. It was a particularly fun evening as it was challenge night.

Everyone who wished to participate made a small quilt or wall hanging in a particular theme. Then all the entries were hung and everyone voted for the one they thought was best. Even as a guest, I was invited to vote. It was wonderful to look at so many original designs and to be welcomed by all the members.

Since then I have become an enthusiastic member myself and participate in challenges and in the quilt show here in Beaufort every two years.

Anne Louttit - "Earthstar"

The Guild was started to promote friendship and to learn quilting. I feel so strongly about this wonderful bunch of women who do so much for the community and who have become such good friends.

St. Helena Island Artisans

Excerpts from 1995 interviews by Diane Dunham

Expressions In Indigo & Ibile Indigo House

Expressions in Indigo and the Ibile Indigo House are the brainchildren of Arianne King-Comer, a visionary who dreamed of celebrating the Gullah culture. She envisioned a wise old oak tree representing St. Helena Island's venerated 'Meeting Place Tree' surrounded by indigo-dyed baskets and fish-nets, indigo quilts and even an indigo bateau - all crafted by local artisans and sheltered by the extraordinary oak tree.

"In my vision I saw this oak tree sculpture as a life sized creation of welded wire sheathed with a skin of indigo fabric bark. ...I found out about the crafts, and who was still doing them here. From that, I figured a good way of honoring the craft people and getting attention to the Penn School, was to have this installation. ... I knew that the final product must involve the talents of many people... other artists."

Her education in the arts and her experiences in West Africa helped her realize her dream. She interviewed local crafts people and encouraged them to participate in her exhibit. Then she designed the fabric, had it indigo-dyed in Nigeria and brought it home to complete the tree.

"I am able to recognize my gift of communicating through art... my art became a spiritual journey. ..." Arianne's long cinnamon-colored dreadlocks frame her radiant face. Her bright eyes and the spatter of freckles across nose and cheeks belie her tremendous spiritual strength.

"As a batik artist I was originally interested in indigo. Once I realized that South Carolina historically was the strongest state for this industry, I wanted to see if the South Carolina leaf was the same (as the Nigerian leaf). In research I found out it was different. I also found out what the differences were in processing. By that time, I was hooked to herbal or natural dyeing from learning how to do it in Nigeria."

Diane Britton Dunham

Studies indicate that when the indigo industry was thriving in the Sea Islands, Indigo was processed chemically using lye and intense heat. Natives of West Africa were brought here by Arianne to teach us how to process our unique variety of indigo leaf organically as it is done in Nigeria, thus bringing us the essence of what indigo was but using the organic methods of West Africa. "I knew before I came here that there are many artists like me trying to have the indigo experience. These artists have to travel all over the world to experience this. I thought well... it used to be here and if I were interested in having it here perhaps others would be as well. Since I had to trek all the way to Africa, it would be nice to have it here particularly with Penn Center as a community service organization."

Arianne's first brainchild was born in Nov. 1995 when Expressions in Indigo was installed in conjunction with the Heritage Celebration at the Penn Center. Expressions in Indigo has since visited Washington, D.C., Walterboro, Orangeburg and Hilton Head, SC, as a salute to the Sea Island craft culture.

Ibile Indigo house, her second brainchild, was funded by a cultural Visions Grant of SC Arts Commission in 1998, and is being supported by SC Coastal Community Development Corp. In order for Ibile Indigo House to be accessible to the public and used for educational purposes, it is located in the old Bishop Farm House near the intersection of Rt. 21 and Martin Luther King Drive on St. Helena Island.

Thomas Mack – Quilt-maker and Tailor

Thomas Mack creates tapestries of warmth and vitality by assembling bits of bright colored fabric with the help of an antique sewing machine. Sparked by his imagination, he blends oranges and reds of "Kinte" cloth with indigo blues to produce fire, and his display of magnificent quilts and beautifully tailored garments, turn his home into a kaleidoscope of vibrant colors and textures.

An affable man, eager to please, and generous, one can't help but like Tommy. Some refer to him as the Electric Hawk because his mannerisms are quick and sharp and he is attuned to the smallest detail ready to take flight on a wave of energy.

Sewing is Tommy's passion. " I haven't bought a suit in 50 years," he proclaims proudly. "When I came out of the army, I got into the post office. I had a job, but I didn't have a trade. I asked the question: what can I do? I couldn't do anything. A man should have a trade." Tommy felt he needed a trade, so... he went to school to become a tailor. "I made all of my kids clothes, and suits for my wife. I used to give left over fabric scraps to my mother-in-law, and the senior citizen center for them to make quilts. I used to have so much left over that I decided to make one myself " Now his quilts are all over the world.

"Gullah and quilting goes back. That was a family thing. At the end of the evening after supper, everybody would sit around the fireplace and play some part in quilt making. They would put scraps together and do some cutting before going to bed. It was a necessary thing. They needed that for warmth. It was a family thing and a form of relaxation."

Tommy's quilts are traditionally southern with a new perspective. His inclusion of Indigo and ethnic "Kinte" fabrics summon a return to his African roots, while he embraces modern culture with Jack-o-lantern prints and Christmas motifs.

What is his creative process? "What grabs me," he says with a wide smile. "It's what grabs me, guides me to make it colorful. It is also from experience with people. They look for a color scheme. At first all of my quilts were of American fabric, but colorful. Then I started putting in more ethnic fabrics. Many quilts in the stores, they have a routine. I don't go for that. I mix it all through - melange, like the French. It works and they like it." It takes about three hours for Tommy to put together a quilt once the scraps are selected and cut. The sewing machine he uses is an old and trusted friend. "I bought it In New York, took it home in a taxi cab in 1947 ... and it wasn't new then."

The Dale Quilters

The "Expressions of Indigo" quilt was made by the Dale Quilters who combined a sampling of quilting styles and techniques. Squares made by children include messages and greetings, an imprint for posterity.

The Dale Quilters, also known as Low Country Ladies, is comprised of three African American women.

- Mrs. Grant, the senior of the group, is 82 years old and the mother of 19 children. She is sharp, attentive, and reserved. While she has little to say, she speaks with authority and her word is undisputed.

- Mrs. Ferguson, a neighbor and mother of eight, defers to Mrs. Grant on quilt-making decisions, true to the cultural tradition of honoring elders. A picture of southern gentility, her voice is melodious and soft, and her mannerisms modest. Yet as quilting instructor for the Dale Senior Citizens, she proves herself a leader.

- Ms. Robinson is Mrs. Grant's daughter and a mother of 13. Like her mother, she radiates a special warmth and effervescence.

"We lap quilt. That's how it used to be. We all get together and sit around and make it (the quilt). That's how it was done in the old days. You didn't have large tables to put it all out. You got together and sewed it on your lap. She might be sitting right here, and I'll have part on my lap and she will have part on hers and she might have another part on her lap." Explained Mrs. Ferguson.

Luke Smalls – Net-maker

Luke returned to his roots on St. Helena Island in 1980. Sometime after that he returned to making fish nets, a craft he hadn't done since he was fourteen years old. "I always knew how it was done, I learned from my uncle, but being away for so many years I had to learn again. Reuben taught me... you know that man with the white hair that walks the road." Luke is referring to Reuben Fripp who is a master and a legend in the art of net making and probably the best teacher anyone could have.

Matt Collins, 11th Grade - Beaufort Academy

Luke's movements are relaxed and flowing as he works, but making the nets takes skill and patience. He even makes his own needles, which he intricately carves from pieces of wood. "In the country," he says " you have to learn something... this is what I do, not for profit but as a hobby. There is no market for handmade nets these days, it is simply an art for me." Net-making is a diminishing art form, but Luke is willing to teach anyone who would like to learn.

There is more to Luke Smalls than making nets. He fought in WWII with the Tuskegee Airmen, and proudly displays his hat bearing their insignia. The Tuskegee Airmen were discriminated against at the beginning of WWII, but were eventually given an opportunity to prove their worth. They succeeded magnificently and were honored in a recent film. "My job was that of mechanic, I kept the planes in the air.'"

Jerry Taylor – Basketmaker

"It is a success story, you see what I'm saying? Living in the south... It wasn't a lot for us to get. We had to make do with what we had. I always count my blessings. Girl, it seemed like we were the poorest people in the world, but it was baskets..."

Jerry Taylor sits in a common lawn chair in front of the old store on Route 21 in Frogmore and sews sweet grass baskets. Her handiwork surrounds her as do the passers by stopping to chat.

"This is ours" she exclaims "This isn't like something we did in our spare time; this is how we ate, paid the insurance. We didn't have electricity. ...Out houses and stuff - that's what we had. If you are a northerner you don't know nothing about that. Our lives back in those times were pure hell; there wasn't a bit for us to get. If you. ... if you had any idea where my family came from up until now, but it was baskets that we learned that brought us to where we are today ... something that has been with me from an infant to present day... There was a lot of joy you know, but we came home from school, we had to pump water, you know we had to wash out our socks and stuff like that, we didn't have machines and stuff, we had to wash our little socks. You didn't get but two pair. You had two dresses. That's the way life has been for us. ... You just had to go out there and make a life for yourself... you had to make things happen! It's just like you have to build the bottom of the basket, first make it strong and build it up from there. ... We lived on Highway 17, ... this has become a dying art in these areas ... because people have moved off. They didn't have an abundance of basket weavers in these parts, but we did it. So that's why baskets were in the Mt. Pleasant area. Mt.

Pleasant, not Charleston! Charleston takes the name 'Charleston Basket' because everybody knows where it is, but it's Mt. Pleasant. Each family does a different style. There are certain peoples' baskets that you can look at and know that's their basket. Just like handwriting."

"We didn't know this craft came from Africa, we thought everybody in the world did it. We didn't know we were a unique people." Jerry says with a laugh, and then with seriousness "Be aware that you hold the Low Country in your hands. ...There is nothing easy about this, try it yourself and you'll see."

Jerry's designs come from within and are the result of a creative force that unfolds during the weaving process. Her goal is to one day create a basket so big, that she has to get inside it to finish making it.

Sam Moultrie – Bateau Builder

Sam Moultrie was about eighteen years old when he learned to build a bateau. "I watched somebody do it," he says in his Native Gullah dialect. "Never did it before in my life. Nobody teach me that." He speaks in earnest. "I practiced them, I couldn't get em straight, but the next one? Perfect! And the more I watched, the better I was than the one that built it. Anything you make I do the same!"

" I just love it," Sam continues. "And I went around, and watch, when they take the paint off them ole sail boats, me join ah factory - I learn it from the ole man Joe Mullins here, I started learning. I love it and so..." He pauses and speaks with caution lest he be misunderstood. "I ain't been to no school now! Technically the only school I been to is the third grade. That's it! ... The only school I been to is to watch somebody."

Lawson Inman, 11th Grade - Beaufort Academy

"You give me a sketch that you want a bateau, 14', 15', 18'. The smallest one I build is 8'. I made a boat 80', from the keel to the bow, to the stern - 80' myself. I take a mold, off a 50' boat, I cast three sets. I can take a mold off a 10' and build a 25'." Sam Moultrie at 72 stands proudly near an enormous shrimp boat he was commissioned to repair. His energy and quick wit belie his age. "Got good eyesight, got good health, can do anything, I'm younger than my baby son here." He refers to his son who has not chosen to follow in his father's footsteps.

When asked if there was a master's apprentice to carry on the torch, Sam proudly introduces his apprentice and number one assistant, Emeral. "Now this is a woman, but God knows I rather work with her than a man. You know why? Women love money, women work for money and gonna spend it wisely." Emeral smiles with pride. She is slender and slight of build. One wonders where she gets the strength to wield the heavy tools she must use. One hammer weighs 20 lbs. Sam continues: "Two young men worked for me, and if I didn't have this woman to call on to do the work?" He waves his hand impatiently. "Forget about them!"

Sam and Emeral demonstrate how they repair the boat. They work as a team - with synchronicity and an uncanny ability to finish each others sentences. It is no wonder that they can complete major jobs in one day. Sam is elusive like a Gypsy, yet engaging, warm and earnest. With the appearance of a seafaring man, his dark earnest eyes light up when he talks about building the bateau. His port is wherever he hangs his hat and so is his workshop. To create, Sam only requires the great outdoors - not blue prints or diagrams - just lumber and his tools.

Li'l Devils

The sand gnats flying across the sand,
Coming across a new piece of land,
Then they see something moving
Its body is grooving.
They fly at lightening fast speed,
They need to feed.
I see them coming,
I go running,
I try to flee
But they got me.

Josh Konoza, 7th Grade
Beaufort Academy

Gnats! Gnats!...

There are so many it should be a sin.
Ahhhh! They're in my mouth
and in my nose.
If you leave your windows open
They will be in your bedroom,
kitchen and den.
Quick someone get the hose.
I've lost my clothes
I just didn't understand because my nose
Is so thin.
How did they get in!?
Sand + Gnats = Beaufort, SC

India Waters 7th Grade - Beaufort Academy

Good Neighbor, Sam

By Louanne LaRoche

I clearly remember the first day I met Sam Doyle. It was in 1980. I lived on Hilton Head Island and had recently taken over ownership of The Red Piano Gallery. Nancy Hewitt, a friend and a client said, "Let's take a field trip over to St. Helena Island. I want you to meet an artist whom I think you would enjoy." She didn't tell me anything else about the artist or the kind of work he did. But the day hangs precious in my memory as a major turning point and a milestone for my personal and professional life. I was about to meet Sam Doyle, a man who has since become one of the world's most renowned contemporary folk artists.

Arriving at his place on St. Helena was like suddenly coming around a corner and discovering a circus or carnival. It always excited you. Always, always Sam greeted visitors graciously dressed in suit and tie. My first day, he was standing by a flagpole where the Stars and Stripes waved high above. Below him, a spotted cat weaved with affection around and through Sam's legs. Ancient oaks shaded the yard. White iron headboards of beds implanted in the yard. Bushes. The steps leading to the screen porch of a handmade house fashioned long, long ago. The bright pink exterior of his wife's abandoned cafe served as the "gallery" where he exhibited his paintings and sculptures.

In lectures I now give about Sam Doyle, the artist, I often describe this first encounter and what came afterwards as comparable to the wonderment, joy and visual intoxication of the Christmas mornings of my childhood. It was a place filled with color...imagination...discovery.

I have often described Sam Doyle as an historian. Mainly because he was recording the history and the people who lived, and had lived, on St. Helena Island. He used house paints and painted on big pieces of tin or scraps of wood; he made sculptures from found objects and from tree limbs and roots he found in the woods, giving them new life. Every painting had a story. Sam was capturing a visual history of his life and the life of the people on St. Helena Island. In his unique and unusual way, he was celebrating the personalities, the Gullah history and language. He was paying tribute to his fellow man fulfilling a real need to do this.

Now that folk art —- the art of self-taught people —- has come into the mainstream of the art world, many people talk about the passion that engulfs these artists...the fact that no one can explain why they suddenly begin creating art.

Arianne King-Comer - "Sam Doyle" Batik

Having known Sam Doyle personally for five years, I can say with great certainty that he had a driving need to do this. He had a great love of community. He had great wit. Part of his need can be defined through the conversations we shared over the years. Sam Doyle knew that his community was changing — rapidly and abruptly. He could see it and feel it. He had a love of history and a divine inspiration to document it through his art. This island was a special place; the people who inhabited it were just as special.

Too many times we equate the concept of "history" with major events such as war or events of national or international significance. Yet history is happening every day. Every community has its history; every person and every family has their history. It is woven into the fabric of every day life.

Sam Doyle had a real need to say, "Stop. Look at this! Here's something you should know about. Don't miss this." He wanted those who saw his work to value his community and its history, as well as valuing their own. He had a need to make his own mark, too. And this, for certain, he has done. His legacy will live forever.

Many people believe that Sam Doyle worked in relative isolation on St. Helena Island, never knowing that his art was achieving national notoriety. I'm sure he didn't depend upon celebrity to continue his life's work in art. But he well knew that he was achieving a special kind of greatness. Sam Doyle's art was featured in the first major museum exhibition of self-taught art. Curated by Jane Livingston, this exhibit was at the Corcoran Gallery of Art in Washington. It created a sensation in the art world to be sure. And Sam Doyle was there, in person, to meet President Reagan and Nancy Reagan and other well-known people who attended the opening. His friends on the island even bought him a new white suit just for the event. And he was smiling even more broadly when he returned home to tell about it.

Sam Doyle passed on in 1985, just a few years after the Corcoran exhibition. He continued to paint until the end. Within a few years of his death, I was asked to write a book about Sam Doyle by a Japanese company which was publishing a series of books about some of the world's most famous emerging artists. I gladly did the book as a way of saying "thanks" for having known Sam Doyle.

When Sam created art, he did it for himself, his family, his friends, the State and Nation, his God. He loved life. He loved his country. His work continues to have a life of its own. Those who understand and are uplifted by its presence nurture this life. There is a force in his art that is as bold and raw as the strokes of his brush. It touches the heart because it came from his heart. I am grateful that Sam Doyle had the courage to say his piece — to tell his stories. He embraced those who were different without judgment; he enshrined them in paintings as a sign to all who would look. Good neighbor, Sam. ❦

It's so hot...

I'll just sit and rock
   Rock, rock, rock, rock, rock, rock.
    Now as the shadows of the night creeps upon me — Look! See the fireflies?
    See how they dance to and fro?
   Shhhhhhhhhhhhhhhhhhhhh! Listen, to the crickets and
That big bullfrog by the pond, serenade in — the heat of the night
Ahhhhhhhh! Me and my rocking chair Cool lemon-aide
My corn cob pipe.
Rock, rock, rock, rock, rock, rock, rock

Walter Dennis

Gloria Dalvini

An Old New Friend

Just lately I have found a friend.

Someone who laughs with me

And we can cry together

For our years on earth are near the end.

Our traveled roads were so far apart

Yet the same scenery -

A man, a home and children of the heart.

All cared for by their mother

Who teaches, who cooked, cleaned and lived.

There was no other - - then.

No day-care, no TV, no wild movie.

No fast cars - just put the horse and buggy away.

Crank up the Ford

Let's go to choir practice and 4H meet.

All our blessings, we thank Thee Lord.

The same Lord.

We have been there and done that.

We know what's behind us.

And we have foresight now.

Those in their 40s refuse to see

Or listen when we speak.

My dear friend now - let us love

Laugh and give

A few words of knowledge

To those that live

In the middle of life

This old world is so full

Of war, worry and strife

"To live and let live" - A motto

Being 80 in the 90s is a study.

Hildred Fern Collier

Susan McLendon

Henrietta and Wilhelmina
Age 4

We played each day. We made up our games of cooking leaves in cans for vegetables and sand cakes for bread. We'd put the 'dishes' - old plates and saucers - to our lips and make believe we were having a delicious meal. Crabs and shrimp from the marsh were our meat. Some times a toad would hop our way and hop away when we tried to catch it. We saw snakes too, but we were taught to look at them from far away and never never go near one. It fascinated us the way they squirmed or wiggled and parted the grass as they took flight. We'd wash our feet and hands at the old pump and drink the cool water from deep down in the earth. We'd take turns pumping and catching the cool clear water in our hands to drink. My mother took me away on a long trip and Henrietta and I never saw each other again. I've never seen her again but now I have a new friend who is an octogenarian like me and I like to believe she is Henrietta. Her name is Hildred.

Wilhelmina Mitchell

A Conversation with Uncle Henry on the Back Step

By Wilhelmina Mitchell

Uncle Henry was not feeling well this Sunday morning. He was sitting out on the back step, holding his head in both hands. My aunt and cousin were dressed for church and were going to leave him at home to nurse his headache.

Auntie said that he deserved a headache. "Comin' in 'fore day this mornin', wakin' everybody with his loud singin' of "John Henry.'"

She didn't tell me to get dressed in my "Sunday-best, go- to-meeting clothes," either. She said I could stay home with him, too. I didn't ask to go with them because I wanted to hear some more of "John Henry," and what a mighty man he was. 'Course, I was sorry that he died with the hammer in his hand.

I eased out onto the steps beside Uncle Henry and sat down beside him. I knew deep down inside me that he couldn't stand any noise because he'd grab his head every time he heard a sound, even though the early Sunday sounds were soft and muted. Only the lowing of the cow for her baby, or the crowing of our rooster who had a special perch atop a fence post. It was clear that he was proud because he'd flap both wings.

The air was cool and sweet with the smell of grass and trees until Uncle Henry yawned. Then, I could smell the familiar tobacco and liquor. I knew to keep quiet, but I couldn't resist asking him to sing "John Henry" again, or to tell me how smart Brother Rabbit was, or how sly Brother Fox was.

Uncle Henry was the smartest man in the world. He could answer all my questions, one by one. He even knew which pig was the mama pig and which pig was the papa pig. Or why buzzards circled and circled a spot and finally 'light to tell us something was dead. He knew all the sounds of' the animals in the woods. He could look up at the sun and tell "what time it is."

I enjoyed staying home with him more than going to hear how frightening God was and how he can see everything, even the littlest ant going in and out of its hole. Jesus was al- right because he loved little lambs and children. But God was frightening and would get you!

The Devil was worse. He'd burn you up in his house called Hell. Uncle Henry said Hell was deep down in the ground. That's why you shouldn't dig down too deep; further down than the well. Uncle Henry said if you asked Jesus to talk to God for you everything would be alright. "Jesus is God's Son, you know, and that's why God loves him so."

So, I figured I would talk to Jesus and ask him to help Uncle Henry, and make his head better. Yes, I'd talk to him tonight after I said my "Our Father." After I figured it out, I felt alright.

Uncle Henry thanked me and put his heavy hand on my head I could feel the love coming through his fingers.

Mandy Elias, 12th Grade - Beaufort High School

Sleeping Beauty Awakened

By Akiba Kiiesmira

Living on St. Helena Island my whole being was soaked in beauty. I could feel, see, hear, touch, and imagine so much beauty. Colors on St. Helena are holographically multiplied and vivified. I discovered that shades of green are endless, blue is the color of the lightest and the deepest peace. Shades of amber and gold recharged my will and amplified the pinks and purples. The wonderful sand roads could hold the heat of the sun in summer and make me earthy not dirty. Listening to the easy tide on the sound led my mind to be in synch with the rhythms of the universe.

I soaked in the beauty of the people too. I bet they don't realize how much Mother Nature has raised them up to be good folk — waving and greeting me at every passing — folk helping me out with rides to town and the dump when it was finally important that I go. It was a delight to see people live out their dreams in their dream homes and have good health and insight. The amazing beauty they created with beads, fabric, clay testified to the basic human instinct to create beauty.

I know that the beauty, generosity, strength, of the plant, the four legged, and winged beings have held my hand and guided me on the path of righteousness that I cling to now. It seems that St. Helena was the perfect place for me to first read The Prophet by Khalil Gibran. I needed the direct connection with the land and the people.

When I first arrived on St Helena I reread Gloria Naylor's Mama Day and I read The Slave Narratives of Frederick Douglas. These writings provided the introduction for continued conversations with the water oaks and Spanish moss. I would walk and daydream, and always I would remember. I could feel the energy of a group of us walking down the road covered in ragged long sleeved clothing protecting us from the mosquitoes. I saw the woman and man we passed, and I felt their dreaming — their dream of me walking this same road in full freedom and delight at just being. So in the tradition of Ancestral Visions, I imagined and visualized black children and elders levitating, flying, skipping, twirling along this same sand road — just being!

There is so much beauty around; you'll find it in yourself.

Sandra Baggett

The Yard

By Sandra Baggette

Magnificent moss-draped oaks surrounded by large embankments of azaleas and camellias prompted me to buy "the yard" in Port Royal in May of 1980. Decades of lush growth and beautiful sunsets on Battery Creek created a fantastic setting that I knew would always be exciting to me. It is this connection with nature that revitalizes and inspires me as an artist and gardener.

Thankfully my family felt the same thrill upon arrival in August. However, there was a problem in this ideal setting. The yard was wonderfully large but the house was a bit small for a family of 6. The evolution of remodeling the house and "mother's yard" has been a source of many family stories and shared laughter in the years since we first called the lowcountry "home".

Sandra Baggette "My Place in the Sun"

Why Beaufort is Special

When I go over bridges we can see dolphins in the water playing with each other. It is enjoyable to people. Beaufort has a lot of unique store and fun activities. When you go to the shrimp or water festivals. You can also visit stores like the Cat's Meow, High Cotton or many galleries displaying local artists work. On the way to Hunting Island Beach and Lighthouse, visitors can purchase handmade sweet grass baskets, fresh fruits and vegetables, and local shrimp at roadside stands. There are still lots of exciting things left to discover in Beaufort.

April Jones, 4th Grade
Broad River Elementary

I like the beach especially when it is my mom's birthday because my mom can have a fun time. I also have a camper so we can go camping. Sometimes my mom wants to leave early when there is a storm coming. It also has five places to sleep. My family and I like to go on bike rides together when we go camping.

Lacey Mattix, 2nd Grade
Shell Point Elementary

I like to watch shrimp boats go by in the ocean. I like the waterfront park and the jet skis at the beach. I like it. I like to watch the dolphins chase the sharks. I like to go swimming in the ocean and look at the alligators.

Billy Bonney, 2nd Grade
Shell Point Elementary

One of the things about Beaufort is the beach and the waterfront park. In the summer we have the Gullah Festival at the waterfront park. I like the birds, and the birds have beautiful wings. Their wings are very colorful, too. The beach is fun because the animals are nice. I really like the turtles because sometimes my sister and I and the kids see the turtles lay their eggs.

Jessica Lopes, 2nd Grade
Shell Point Elementary

I like Beaufort because of the animals and the people and the children. I like the water because I can swim. I love the beach because it is fun and I can build sand castles. I like fishing because I can catch sharks and stingrays.

Amber Morgan, 2nd Grade
Shell Point Elementary

I like Beaufort because of the way the alligators growl and fight and the way egrets eat shrimp out of the marshes. I like how the snakes rattle their tails and chase mice. Beaufort is the best.

William Dawson, 2nd Grade
Shell Point Elementary

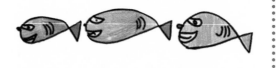

Beaufort

Beaufort is a city in South Carolina. It has a lot of history. It even has history in the slavery history. Beaufort used to be a place where the slaves used to have freedom. A man named Robert Smalls used to be a slave. Robert Smalls is still here in Beaufort. Robert was so famous they named streets and a middle school after him. Beaufort is a small town. It's probably a small town but it has a lot of history. My mommy and my daddy lived here all their childhood life. Beaufort has a beach called "Hilton Head Beach." It has a lot of sticky stuff on it. Hilton Head Beach has a lighthouse by it. I went in it before and it was scary. I went to the top. I really like Beaufort because it is peaceful.

Janay Glover, 5th Grade
Broad River Elementary

Alan Dehls

Beaufort

Beaufort is a nice place.
Most of the year it's hot.
They have a fair that comes once a year.
Beaufort has a Water Festival in June.
They also have a Gullah festival.
At the water festival you can play games.
They have races like raft racing, sail boat
racing and they even have bed races.
They have concerts for kids and adults.
They have a talent show.
They have a special night where we get to
see fire works.

Matthew Tate, 4th Grade
Broad River Elementary

Brittney Johnson, 5th Grade - Broad River Elementary

Ethan James, 4th Grade - Mossy Oaks Elementary

The Waterfront

Beaufort is a very lovely place. I like the Water
Front Park the best. There are a lot of birds and sun-
shine. Every year there is a fair called the Water
Festival. There are races for boats, arts and crafts,
games, face paintings, and a whole lot more. It is very
fun. There is a marine boat that you can go in and
check it out. On the boat there is a machine gun and
one bullet would blow you a mile away! The Water
Front is a beautiful place and it is filled with grass,
trees, flowers, and very fresh air. The Water Front
Park is down town. I bet you'll find it by how beautiful it is!

Ethan James, 4th Grade
Mossy Oaks Elementary

Jessica Baker, 4th Grade, St. Helena's Elementary

Students listed in index (M-W)

Florence Yuen, while attending Beaufort High School

Call It A Love Story

By Nancy M. Gebhardt

The ayr is clear and sweet, the country very pleasant and delightful.
Captain William Hilton, 1663

We weren't the first or the last Yankees to fall in love at first sight with Hilton Head Island. Coming as we did from cities and suburbs, we were astonished to see the deep pine forests and burly live oaks, festooned with moss — a *wilderness* that was halted by a broad sweep of beach. We explored the wave-trimmed rim of the Island, followed trails ending in marshland, meandered on sandy roads through the silent forest where light filtered down on secrets of the past. We stood in Nature's cathedral. Towering beauty was commonplace here.

This 1959 encounter with the Island was during the time Carl was stationed with the U. S. Navy in Charleston. We began packing up our young family and small dog in the VW and driving to Hilton Head on weekends. At least once we pitched a tent on the beach for the night, only to find that a population of plump, nocturnal spider crabs had prior claim to the campsite. By 1961 we were building our compact, innovative home in Palm Forest across from South Forest Beach. We had terrazzo floors throughout, a cathedral ceiling, a fishpond in our step-down living room, Hilton Head Island's only sunken bathtub, and hand-cut cypress shakes on our roof. Eighteen hundred square feet for under $10,000!

We were still in the first wave of pioneers and involved in building an elegant beachfront resort, the Adventure Inn. It opened in 1963 during the tricentennial of Hilton Head Island, namesake of Captain William Hilton. We named our inn after his "good ship Adventure." The resort project turned out to be a crash

Carla Wynn, 11th Grade - Beaufort High School

course in business administration: design and construction, interior decoration, hotel and restaurant management, personnel housing and training programs.

Early resort development on Hilton Head was entrusted to a rare gathering of people who were guided by environmental and aesthetic sensibilities. The creative mix of energy, talent and vision made living on the island an extraordinary experience. Trend-setting architecture and land-use plans seemed to inspire Hilton Head's signature lifestyle – low-key, but high-tone. The Island attracted artists, writers, intellectuals as well as businessmen, builders, sportsmen and naturalists. The fabric of social life consisted of oyster roasts, tennis matches, cocktail parties, impromptu barbecues as well as bird walks, mini think tanks, beautification and conservation meetings. Everyone on the Island wore a few extra hats. The young Chamber of Commerce nominated Carl to wear the president's. We both witnessed or were active in the launching of the Audubon Society, the Island Film Society, a chapter of the Coastal Zone Mental Health Association, the Hilton Head Historical Society, Garden Club, Head Start, Planned Parenthood and a Kindergarten Co-op. With reasonable effort anything seemed possible. In fact I ran for the Beaufort County School Board in 1963 and got one serendipitous write-in vote for U. S. President.

During those early years we often saw Nature in the raw. Our Siamese cat made daily deliveries of her trophies — fresh livers, entrails and such — on our doorstep. We stumbled upon lethargic copperheads sunbathing in the freshly turned earth; we were wakened at midnight to the snorting of wild boars rooting grubs out of our pine-straw driveway. Our dachshund disappeared into the nearest lagoon, or rather, into the granddaddy alligator who patrolled that territory.

One fabulous night in June we had the rare good luck to come upon a nesting loggerhead. We stayed for the whole show while the huge turtle laid her eggs, covered them with sand and dragged herself across the wide beach to sink beneath the waves. Only by this time our flashlight batteries were also exhausted, and the moon had set. It was pitch black and a long and disorienting ordeal to find our way home, bruised, scratched, and humbled by the experience. In 1964 we raced across the drawbridge in a gathering hurricane to birth our baby in the relative safety of Beaufort Memorial Hospital. Nothing about living here was ho-hum.

Hilton Head was always a magnet for family and friends. Summer times were for shucking corn and cleaning crabs and shrimp by the gross —for sharing our space with visitors and keeping up with grandparents, brothers, sisters, cousins. But there was a fateful blow in store for us. One cold

January, before we could get her to the hospital, we lost our seven-year-old daughter to viral pneumonia. Our exuberance and optimism suddenly fell silent, and in time we decided to leave the Island.

Carl joined the CIA. It was a one-hundred-eighty degree change and a good one for us. During his twenty-six-year career we lived in Washington and five other world capitals: Mexico City, Warsaw, Bangkok, Jakarta and Moscow. Each new assignment was an education and a challenge, adding more excitement and adventure to our lives than we ever imagined possible. But, from time to time, we missed the beach. We sought out some famous ones at Acapulco, Puerto Vallarta, Skiathos, Pattaya, and Bali. In a pinch we even settled for the banks of the Moscow River where we learned how much even a bad beach can mean to sun-and-fun-starved people.

Naturally we drew comparisons. In our quarter-century personal survey Hilton Head Island's beach was simply unbeatable. We found that the best and most beautiful beach in the world is right here in a corner of Beaufort County which so influenced our early married life and still has a hold on us. When we retired in 1992 we made a beeline for Hilton Head.

Things are not the same of course. For one thing the roads are paved. We don't wave at every car that goes by; most of the drivers are strangers. Not only is traffic heavy, it's a heavy topic. But we are satisfied that resort development, which was bound to be an intrusion for some even as it was an opportunity for others, has been held to decent bounds. It is civilized here, even cosmopolitan — and still beautiful.

It has been easy to find new friends here. There are hundreds of congenial choices — ways to enjoy nature, to be entertained, to be educated, to serve the community, to bask in quiet solitude. Once again we are visited by family and friends. Our children love this place. And we feel a deep sense of homecoming every time we salute the resident alligator in his lagoon or watch a flock of pelicans fly low over the waves when we bicycle down the broad, bountiful beach. The colors, the climate, the easy pace, the sense of history and, above all, the light slanting across the water drew us back here to stay for good.

Ryan Walker, 4th Grade

M.C. Riley Elementary

83

Eric Horan

Where's Your Horse, Abe?

By Joe Adams

Coming out of the hardware store recently, I saw Abe getting into an old but beautifully restored red Ford convertible. I hollered, "Where's your horse, Abe?" At first he had a puzzled look on his face. Then he smiled broadly, shrugged his shoulders and said sadly. "Vanished."

Abe's black. A successful man of color. On Hilton Head Island, we usually refer to black people as Native Islanders. We do it sort of in honor of their role of being here long before the transplanted, yet we know damn well that the Indians were here first. But they're no longer around to honor. And neither are the Marsh Tackies, Abe's unique breed of horse. Vanished. Not quite like the Indians, but gone nevertheless.

When I first started coming to Hilton Head Island on a regular basis more than twenty years ago, I would see Abe's horse staked out in a field by his roadside restaurant, Abe's Shrimp House. The horse had become as much a landmark as the rickety old drawbridge that occasionally got stuck open and leaves us stranded. We yearned to get onto the island if we were stranded on the Bluffton side of the river; didn't care if the bridge ever got unstuck if we were on the island side. We were more than eager to stay forever.

My children felt sorry for Abe's horse — partly for the way he looked, partly for the fact that he seemed to live in the same spot, month after month. But the horse seemed happy enough. He wasn't pretty as horses go. He had a big head. He was short, probably no more than five and a half feet tall. His big ears made me think of the mules my grandfather used to plow South Carolina cotton fields when I was a boy. Still, even on the end of the rope and looking sort of dopey, the horse had a certain elegance about him. Mainly he looked displaced as cars whizzed by on the island roadway.

Once I was finally able to stay forever on Hilton Head Island, the Marsh Tacky horses began to fascinate me. Maybe it was because I had taken my young children to Chincoteague Island in Virginia to see the wild shipwrecked ponies that have continued to live and breed there for a hundred years or more. Or maybe it was because I had a keen vision of the wild horses I had seen galloping in the surf's edge on Cumberland Island in Georgia. But if I told the God's honest truth, more than likely it was because I had read about a rich guy in Kentucky who was trying to start a whole new sporting event — indoor horse racing in arenas all over the country. You couldn't race regular sized horses on an indoor track, but this guy had a special breed of small, fast horses. He figured he would have all the winners since he was the only one known to have small, fast horses. Yeh, well he had never heard of the Marsh Tacky or its propensity for flat out racing. My dream was to find and breed Marsh Tackies; get a whole stable of horses and show up at the opening of the first indoor horse race and take all the prize money! Sure it was a stupid dream. But that's what men do in their minds. Come up with stupid dreams, then give them up. I've given up more dreams than I can remember, but it's been fun chasing a few.

Everybody I talked to about the Marsh Tacky told me stories of their natural competitive bent; about how the black families would gather on Sundays after church and have an island version of the Kentucky Derby; how at Christmastime, no matter how far off people had wandered, they'd come back home, eat a lot and race the Marsh Tackies on Christmas Day. Racing during the holidays was as commonplace as Christmas trees.

The feisty speed of the Marsh Tacky gave me a dream worthy of chase. I was already designing race silks in my mind. Maybe something with the color of marsh grass at the height of summer. Or gold, the way it turns in the fall.

Searching the island here, I only found a couple of aging Marsh Tackies left. Like Abe's horse, they were usually staked out. Emory Campbell told me he still had one, but it was a family keepsake. Mike Cohen still had his prized Starbright, one of the fastest of the Marsh Tackies in prime. (Poor thing got bitten by a rattlesnake later and died.)

It became readily apparent that the Marsh Tackies were becoming a vanishing breed. The few remaining horses no longer ploughed the fields. Nobody rode them bareback to the post office anymore. The mail was being delivered now. But whenever I would talk to any black man on the island about Marsh Tackies, his face would light up. These men didn't just grin when they talked about the horses. Lots of times they would laugh out loud as they remembered and re-told their youthful exploits on the back of a Tacky.

One man told me, "They were crazy about running and racing. Had a competitive streak and they were fast as lightning. We raced up and down the roads. Every family had one; sometimes two or more."

In fact, island records show that the Marsh Tackies numbered more-than a hundred when developers first arrived on Hilton Head Island. Further back they may have numbered a thousand or more. Documents from the aftermath of the Civil War indicate that black families were given "forty acres and a Marsh Tacky" along with their freedom.

Although the Marsh Tacky's existence was first noted after the Civil War, the horses had been on the island for many, many years before.

Todd Ballentine, a naturalist and expert on the environment, thinks the horses probably came in the late 1400's, survived on marsh grass which worked sort of like a salt block providing them with fresh water, sodium and roughage.

But the great and continuing mystery is how they got here in the first place.

Romantics would have us believe the Marsh Tackies were Andalusians that swam to shore after an off-coast Spanish shipwreck, then lived in Robinson Crusoe fashion in their newfound island paradise waiting for someone to show up and give them gainful employment.

While the Marsh Tacky has features that are reminiscent of Andalusians, most authorities doubt this origin of ancestry.

We know for certain that the Seminoles had horses of Spanish descent. And even English thoroughbreds were appearing in South Carolina by the late 1700's. Wealthy planters brought down Morgan horses from the north and they're a breed that's tough, small and fast. No wonder there's speculation that the Marsh Tacky may have come from a mixture of horses, thus explaining their odd but sometimes elegant features. But, who knows?

Another school of thought has the horses arriving even before Christopher Columbus hit America; coming to the Sea Islands with the first settlement on Santa Elena, near Paris Island. Theory goes the horses were left by the settlers who mysteriously disappeared. Serious historians laugh at the idea: "They ate their horses! And the settlers may have been eaten, too."

If there's disagreement on how the horses got here, there's nearly as much about how they got their names. Not so much the "marsh" part since they were known to graze on marsh grass. It's the "tacky" part that's in slight dispute. It didn't come from their appearance because they were much too well loved for anybody to call them tacky looking. Black people say the name comes from the Gullah word taki, meaning a small horse. Others say tacky means an inferior or wild horse, like a feral. (Tackle is also a South African word for sneakers, which has nothing to do with horses.) I personally lean toward the Gullah idea because I don't know of a soul who would ever admit that the Marsh Tacky had a single inferior quality. Everyone who's owned one has nothing but praise for them.

As plough horses, they would work the fields from sun-up to sundown, never tiring or acting mule-headed. They had the stamina to get any job done that required a workhorse. Yet they also allowed themselves to be hitched to a wagon or buggy for carrying island families; or to be ridden bareback through the bramble and brush, across a salt marsh and to the post office. Come Sunday, there was yet another metamorphosis into a brilliant racing steed. No! There was nothing tacky about a Marsh Tacky. Small in size, as the Gullah word implies, but a giant heart and soul.

Now, they've vanished. Any that remain are too old to breed; too tired to run; too weak to plough. Keepsakes until their time comes to vanish. And, so goes my own dream of seeing them race and win.

(Endnote: But wait! For those who fear the Marsh Tacky has truly vanished, good news! Rest easy. They've vanished from Hilton Head Island. But like many who get crowded out when development spreads, a whole herd of Marsh Tackies is thriving in Jasper County. They're there because of another man's dream. One that he fulfilled. They're under the loving care of D.P. Lowther who now has more than 30 Marsh Tackies. He treats them as pets, not workhorses. He's determined to keep the breed alive. And it's not because of the whacky idea of indoor arena horse racing. He does it because he loves them.)

Jennie Ross, 4th Grade - M.C. Riley Elementary

Reading at the Dynamo Cafe

(for Chick Ash)

The tall bloke with the Seamus Heaney bulk and a warm smile
whispered blue voodoo lagoons of Gullah heat and hunger;
of hands learning how to block out color, and stock in
the Frogmore Funnel of stew-baked landlore,
and we all leaned forward, biting hard on hearing,
hearing easy loam-fed richness of expression
to out-Heaney the man himself: a chapel of ease,
centered and diligent, gentle and sibilant, wishing
language at the well of gauged words spent in awe
of the weed-draped shorelines sliding sure-foamed up the coast.
No shrimp, this; shark-tongued and alert, por-poised on the edge,
on the very gunwales of the flying spray-decked page:
sailing home and taking us with him, eager for every word
in the ash-light evening's slow pull of welcome, winsome telling.

Sheila Tombe

Tales of the Tin Palace

By Laura Von Harten

My family's first home in Beaufort was a ramshackle tin-clad two story garage on Lady's Island. It had been built in 1926 by my father's uncle, Willie Roberts. Kinfolk who had lived and worked there dubbed it "The Tin Palace."

The building was worn out from 40 years of hard use by the time we moved in. It smelled of pitch and fish and mold. The bottom floor, modified for use as living space in the 1940s, was converted into a fish market for my father's wholesale and retail seafood business. My parents set up housekeeping on the second floor.

A steep wooden staircase, with a wall on either side, connected the first and second stories. The passage led from the windowless cleaning room, with its fish-gutting smells and cold concrete floors and transistor radio blare, to our slightly more comfortable quarters above. At the top of the stairs lay a narrow landing barely large enough for one person. Its window was the only one that overlooked the shrimp dock and packinghouse on Factory Creek.

The window was my favorite place for tossing breakfast leftovers to eager seagulls whose antics were a source of unending delight. It was also, literally, my window onto the world. With the dual hazards of deep water on one side, and Highway 21 on the other, roaming the grounds was not an option for a preschooler. So it was from this tin tower that I surveyed the elements of my life spread out below me like a soft and distant quilt.

That tiny landing was my favorite place to spend time, but it had the potential to be as dangerous as the creek or the highway. In order to reach the window I had to perch precariously on a chair whose legs came perilously close the edge of the top step. I needed the cooperation of an adult who would hold the chair and protect me from plunging down that precipitous flight of stairs.

One morning I careened off of the landing. The chair and I began a bruising cartwheel down the dusty, narrow steps. I was terrified, of course, but it scared my grandfather even more. His name was Larry Butler, but everyone called him Captain Butler. He lived in Doane's Trailer Park, directly across from us on Highway 21. He had brought his trailer up from Key West and parked it at the rented lot until years later, when he moved it next door to the fish market. The trailer had faulty wiring, so sometimes when you crossed over the threshold you'd get an unpleasant shock. It didn't bother Capt. Butler.

My grandfather was usually out fishing, but on that particular day he was supposed to be looking after me while my parents were working below. He was strong and leather-tan from years of fishing in the Tortugas, and when I tumbled down the stairs he raced to catch me before I crashed to the bottom. After tears were spilled and expressions of concern uttered, we found there was no harm done. Before long I had returned to my position on the chair in the landing and was surveying my domain once again.

The docks were at the end of a driveway that stretched a hundred yards toward the water from Highway 21. There was enough room for two cars or one large truck on the oyster shell drive, which was not the usual mixture of sand and soil topped with a thin layer of shells. As with many working waterfronts in the Sea Islands, this one had expanded over the decades. An accumulation of shells and debris, much of it deliberately placed, had been covered by organic matter until it became integrated into the landscape, and assumed the status of deedable land. A portion of our property was real estate of this order.

West of the docks, in the betwixt-and-between space between land and water, was a sort of grave-yard of material goods. Like all graveyards it held memories as well as physical remains. Along with

Walter Dennis

92

miscellaneous household and industrial debris, there was my grandfather's wooden shrimp boat, the G. Phillip Maggioni, that had been punctured at dead low tide by a decrepit piling hidden beneath the surface of the water.

The boat had been built in Thunderbolt, GA, for a man named Paul Cesaroni. Cesaroni was a shrimp cannery manager for Maggioni & Company. When his contract with them expired in the 1930s he started his own dock on Lady's Island, down at the end of Sam Point Road. After a stint in the Cesaroni fleet in Beaufort, the G. Phillip Maggioni ended up in Key West, where Capt. Butler bought it. The boat ended up back in Beaufort in the 1960s after Capt. Butler decided he wanted to be closer to his daughter. So in one of those strange twists of fate, the G. Phillip Maggioni ended up being buried within miles of where it had shrimped at the beginning of its career.

Its subterranean neighbor in this heap of trash becoming land was my grandfather's old Nash station wagon. Capt. Butler would drive me and my brother, Bo, on outings to the end of Meridian Road. There was no McTeer Bridge at that time, so the pavement came to an abrupt stop. We let the dogs, Gus and Pongo, out to run, and my brother and I would walk around and marvel at the fact that a paved road could simply end, just like that. It seemed like the edge of the earth.

What was even more amazing to us was the fact that when we rode in the Nash, we could see large sections of the road rushing beneath our feet. Gaping holes in the rusty floorboard threatened to give way at any moment, and we kept our feet up on the seat for fear that we would fall through. We were always glad to get back home to the relative safety of the Tin Palace.

The docks were off limits to me when I was very young, so mostly I viewed them from

Walter Dennis

afar. Because I was not in the thick of the noise and sweat and smell of the place, the docks impressed me as being beautiful and mysterious. Shrimp boat masts towered above the roof of the packing house. Each boat was festooned with colorful nets, floats, and "hula skirts" - pieces of party-colored fringe that trimmed the whole ensemble like a feather boa. The saturated tones of sky and water were punctuated by spiky spartina grass, worn wooden pilings, and rusted metal machinery. Jagged bits of oyster shell covered every inch of the ground, except in the places where climbing vines covered the shell.

In the afternoon and late into the night the dock hummed with activity. Shrimpers cleaned their boats and made phone calls and kept an eye out while their catch was processed. While they were waiting for the boats to come in, the headers played cards on improvised outdoor gaming tables made from rope spools and overturned crates. Trucks laden with huge blocks of ice arrived and other trucks full of shrimp departed for the breading factories down south. The big picture was exciting, but the people were the best part.

There was Arabelle, who headed shrimp, and had a regal face and what I thought was the most beautiful name in the world. Rena was old and wizened, with her head wrapped in the old time Gullah style, and whiskers emerging from a resolute chin that bobbed up and down as she talked. I couldn't understand a word she said. Andrew Johnson, the pensive dock manager who was no doubt embarrassed by my insistence that he was my best friend, wore intriguingly large Mexican sombreros. He would haul shrimp in the big trucks, and would return from trips to Key West bearing Cuban bread and other tropical delicacies. Andrew Myers, who had come up on a boat from St. Mary's and ended up staying in Beaufort for the rest of his life, worked at first in the boatyard, then helped manage retail operations at the fish market.

We sold beer in the fish market, so there was plenty of drunken trouble making from intoxicated islanders until my father became a Christian and decided to do away with the alcohol. There were other things for sale too: milk, sodas, Vienna sausages, sardines, crackers, candy, cigarettes, and basic marine supplies. When I was a baby I was stationed in a playpen among the shelves, and as I got older I could stay by myself, looking at books, in the rooms upstairs. If I needed anything, all I had to do was walk to the room above my parents' office and rap briskly on the ceiling.

After my sister Tracy came along the apartment started to seem crowded. Bo and I shared a bedroom, and Tracy had a crib in the living room. Then, when a fourth child was on its way in 1969, my parents decided it was time to move. They found a solid brick house in Hundred Pines, a suburb of Beaufort. It had three bedrooms and a fenced yard and room for the dogs to run. But in my eyes there was plenty that was missing: water, docks, seagulls, the endless parade of people.

Needless to say I didn't like it when we moved to town. It was partly because I was worried that my mother wouldn't be able to find us. She was in the hospital giving birth when my father organized the move. I was sure she didn't know where our new home was. I imagined her going back to the apartment on Lady's Island, finding it empty and roaming about town like a ghost.

The worst part of moving to town was being cut off from the flow of activity on Lady's Island. I missed my father's enthusiastic smile and the way he rubbed his hands briskly together as he bounded up the stairs during a break from work. When we ran out of milk it seemed strange not to be able to dash downstairs for another carton.

Walter Dennis

There was no doubt our standard of living improved after the move. There was a boys' bedroom and a girls' bedroom, and closets. It had a good fuel oil heater that vented warm air throughout the house, so the water didn't freeze in the toilet bowl on the coldest of nights as it had at the old place. Best of all, we had more room to take care of the kittens that were a never-ending presence in our household. People would dump cats at the market, and the cats had myriad kittens. Some we caught and tamed and gave away, and others remained wild on the property.

The house in town was my parents' pride and joy, but as I was growing up the Tin Palace on Lady's Island remained the center of our family life. My parents spent most of their time working at the fish market, and my brothers and sister and I worked there too when we weren't in school. My mother eventually opened a restaurant next to my father's fish market. Much to the amusement, and at times, chagrin, of the other employees, family dramas usually played out in the sanctity of the home made their way to the workplace instead.

My parents sold the place in the late 1980s after all of the children had gone off to college. They got regular jobs with health benefits, paid holidays, and the promise of small pensions. The new owners renovated the Tin Palace, covered it with blue siding, and turned it into a restaurant and unwitting monument to the Sea Island's transition to a tourism and retirement oriented economy.

Almost every trace of industry was removed from the property. Of course they left the dock; even as it deteriorated, its presence would grandfather-in a new dock and guarantee it could be built with a minimum of paperwork. For some reason they left the shell of an old freezer, and painted the cube with a mural of two men fishing. Each time I see the painting I think about the two men who used to live inside that old freezer. They had all the comforts of home in their small household - couch and bed, TV and dog. One of the men received letters from a government agency; they were addressed to him at "Von Harten Seafood, Condo #1 (freezer out back), Beaufort, SC, 29902."

Bryan Larsen, 3rd Grade
M.C. Riley Elementary

Natural Beauty

The backroad takes me through
The heart of the lowcountry.
Away from the salty marsh,
Into the swamp-black back waters.

The ground is soggy from rainfall,
But, the sun is out.
Nice and hot
The first week of March.

The weather has drawn you out
Of your modest home.
A cypress clad dwelling
Blackened by age.

You, young lady, a beautiful sight.
Passing by at the speed of light

I catch a glimpse of your delicate white
Body clad in blue denim dress
Hiding what is sure to be the best
Of what nature has to offer.

You, young lady, in the garden plot
Readying the rows for
Green beans and summer squash.

Oblivious to your highway admirers
If your back was not turned
I'm sure you would have waved.
Most do in this area,
Where the swollen black rivers
Flow through bald cypress stands.

Kirk Dempsey

Anthony Smalls, 10th Grade *Computer Enhanced*

The Settlement

I am a vagabond, moving from place to place. Words and images flood my mind, a tide that won't stop long enough to be dammed. A tide that takes my thought back out to sea, lost to me. It is unsettling this settling of land and sea.

Barrier islands, barrier gates, barrier fences. What are the barriers, fencing me out, them in? Settlements of people looking for refuge? Barriers are two-sided. They both protect and they threaten, they provide a haven and they destroy a haven. Where is my home? I have become a wanderer in my own front yard.

Melba Cooper

Shalonda Bryan- Beaufort High School

Caryl Sweet - "The Tree House at Pritchards Island"

Jorge Otero - "Chapel of Ease"

Living on the Edge

By Benton Lutz

My family and I recently moved to Beaufort, South Carolina, a town of seafaring vagabonds - people who find this seaport on their travels and because of its beauty, drop their anchors permanently. We are at home with these people. They live on the edge, on the margins of maps and charts. They don't share inlanders' illusions of stability. They are aware the next storm could wash them away. This seems to cause an unhurried urgency to take care of what needs caretaking.

Down at the waterfront several restaurants offer tables on porches that take advantage of the view. Cats roam those porches begging for food. One particular cat, dressed in a tux with white spats, is hard to deny.

The town jester, Tootie, sweeps a few blocks of sidewalk with a Lion's Club broom, picking up cigarette butts and trash. He got hit by a car soon after we moved here, and the hospital was so overwhelmed by calls about him that they had to install a Tootie hot-line.

There are guys down at the waterfront who, when they're off work, spend most of the night throwing nets into the dark, rushing brine. They talk, share supplies, and display unique casts which usually involve putting part of the net in their teeth. It's at least as tricky as a fly rod, equally messy if not done right. It can look as tangled as original sin.

A woman I'll call Sara lives at the end of our street. Her yard is a collection of cinder blocks, dead potted plants, shopping carts, old TVs - a graveyard of commercialism, decomposing corpses of every imaginable thing. Sometimes you can see her sitting among her things wondering what to do next. I know the feeling.

A young woman walks by the shrimpers who are casting like disciples. "Hi, Doc, how you doin' tonight?" they greet her warmly.

"Fine, Charles," she says to one of them, "How's the catch?"

"They showin' their mean side tonight, Doc," Charles replies.

Jerry Eskridge, Beaufort High School

"Least they're showing you something," she smiles back. She spies Tux, who looks up expectantly but warily, her white feet poised in that prim way cats have of sitting like debutantes. "How's the begging business?" Doc asks as she digs into her pockets for some dry cat food.

As she walks away, Charles, who has on other nights, tried to teach me to cast a net, says, "One hell of a Doc."

"Really, she's a doctor?"

"Oh, yeah. Stitched my leg back together after a shark like to tore it off," he says. "Comes down here almost every night to feed the cats just in case the day's begging hasn't been too prosperous."

The edges seem to attract a certain intensity, like the rim of a cloud with the sun behind it, or the moon during a lunar eclipse. Here on the banks of the Beaufort River, a few watery miles from the Atlantic Ocean there are some strangely intense people, unafraid of rim-light.

I recently took a class and met Jack Kerouac - reincarnate. He is busy redefining the world one word at a time, putting his poignant definitions on T-shirts, which sell like hotcakes. "Jack" had a little angry outburst in class - as sometimes happens with the true geniuses among us. He was complaining about all that is wrong with Beaufort when a native said, "If you are that unhappy, why don't you leave?"

Jack thought for a moment and said, "The trees."

This is a town of centuries - old live oaks so hallowed that streets go around them. City council recently put out a request for bids for software that would inventory the street trees. Jack may not like the people here, but he loves the trees.

It's not just the people who are a bit off-kilter. The plants and animals live like Tootie, Sara, Charles and Doc. They do the best they can in the place they are planted.

Resurrection ferns, for example, live on the majestic branches of live oaks but they are only along for the ride, since they live on air. The ferns turn as dark as pluff mud when we go without rain for a few days. But as soon as there is any rain at all, they spring back to life. There is a kind of marsh grass that eats mosquitoes. There is also a fish that eats mosquitoes. Both are plentiful since mosquitoes are so plentiful. There are all kinds of root and berries that will cure anything, or if not used properly, cause anything - which makes the local voodoo doctors indispensable. There are milk snakes in our front yards, Carolina Wrens who sleep on our porches, and Marines who fly overhead in F-18s. This is where Forrest Gump jumped off Miss Jenny and where no self-respecting disciple would be without his Bubba Gump hat while casting his net.

Whether we realize it or not, we are all spiritual vagabonds. Living on the edge of some place helps us keep that reality in mind. We are all traveling some watery way, trying to understand what life is all about. We struggle to learn what our responsibilities are to each other, to stray cats, to those who fill their yard with castoffs, to historic street trees, to the creative genius among us who struggles with some private demon and writes the world a love note on T-shirts, and to those caught in the jaws of sharks.

We are all living on the air. And like the resurrection fern that lives in the mighty arms of massive trees, we are basically along for the ride on this fragile planet. We look as dead as dirt when nutrients are denied and as healthy as saints when we are nourished. We sleep on porches huddled in corners like Carolina wrens, feathers ruffled to keep out the cold. We beg for food like Tux and her friends. We trust an ancient use of root and berries called modern medicine.

Some of us do what we can to make things better. Like Tootie, we sweep the street on which we find ourselves until something strikes us down. We all know that we could be blown away in the next hurricane. We anchor as best we can.

From an article published in 1996, in "The Other Side" a magazine of Justice, Peace and Discipleship.

Evelyn Mitchell, while attending Lady's Is. Middle

The Wonders of Beaufort

There are many wonders in Beaufort, S.C. like downtown, Beaufort. There are many historic buildings and houses. There are many stores and restaurants. Even though its old, its still pretty.

Michele Horne, 4th Grade
Mossy Oaks Elementary

A Contemplation On Empyrean Peregrination

By Brewster Milton Robertson

Sheer chance? ... Or a converging of planetary alignments and mystical cosmic gravitation?

Looking back over the two dozen years since that unforgettable day in 1974 when I first fell under Beaufort's magic spell, I guess I should have had some cobwebbed precognition that I was fated to return to this South Carolina island-dotted paradise.

I grew up in Salem, Virginia, a small college town in the foothills of the Appalachian Mountains near Roanoke. As a child, my universe took shape amid the dusty stacks of books in the drafty old building where my Aunt Blanche founded the county library. Even before I started first grade, it was there that I first dared dream I might grow up to live the writing life.

While attending a convention one magical spring day in 1974, 1 found myself footloose ... exploring ... island-hopping my carefree way across the thirty-odd picturesque miles transversing the long bridges and winding roads from postcard-perfect Hilton Head Island. I shall never forget that first time I turned into the heart-stopping cathedral of grandfatherly moss-bearded live oaks running along Bay Street, overlooking the Beaufort River with its picture-book harbor. In the quaint business district, perfect strangers smiled and waved.

I was spellbound that day in 1974 when I stumbled onto Beaufort. That unforgettable afternoon, I became hopelessly enthralled. In that moment, Beaufort forever put its mark on me. I had no inkling then that twenty years would pass before I would find myself helpless to resist its seductive call.

During the two decades that followed, like the nearsighted Mr. Magoo, I stumbled around from place to place, oblivious that we are all skating on the rim of utter chaos. Over that span of my driven existence, meandering through the Carolinas, Virginia, Washington, DC, back to the Carolinas, Florida and back again, I took turns as teacher, photographer's model, film actor and copywriter.

Through it all, I wrote ... still dreaming that someday I would live the writing life. Gradually my writing began to appear in journals and magazines. Incredibly, I became a consulting editor and was offered work as a ghostwriter though I was almost unaware; my reputation as a literary critic had grown in baby steps.

By 1992 I had written a novel and found an agent ... a well-known Brit who foolishly believed I hung the literary moon ... or so he said. Like any schoolboy, I was so eager to believe him that, not having a clue where I would find my next sou, I resigned my job and found myself making grand plans to live out my dream.

Like postcards from another lifetime, I believe that each of us has genetically double-helixed deep into our protoplasm mystical predilections for certain places ... places we have never seen or heard of before. Who among us hasn't stepped off a plane in a completely alien place or turned down an unknown lane to find ourselves visited by the eerie feeling that this is where we were always meant to be?

So, it was on a fine day in the spring of 1993, the second time I glided under the breathtaking bower of grandfatherly moss-bearded live oaks running along Bay Street, overlooking the Beaufort River with its storybook harbor. This time I was leading a mover's van. It was as if time had stood still. Wafting the exotic essence of pungent salt marsh mixed with jasmine and honeysuckle, the air was intoxicating. Dogwoods and azaleas abounded. Thick ropy vines of wisteria embraced the majestically soaring pines, dripping bejeweled splashes like amethyst waterfalls. Even butterflies seemed to have a magic air of Technicolor perfection. Had I somehow stepped inside the borders of a Maxfield Parrish illustration or perhaps a film by Disney?

Today, I am a full-time writer/novelist/teacher/literary critic. Incredibly, all of this has come true since I came to Beaufort six years ago dreaming of slaying literary dragons.   It's not every man who can live inside his fantasy ... in this delightful realm that nurtures me.

Roger Camelo

Carla Wynn

Meggie Rushton

...while attending Lady's Island Middle School

Essence Of Beaufort
The Creative Arts

By Ethard Wendel Van Stee

I. My Odyssey

After living in Chapel Hill for 20 years, I'd had enough of North Carolina. Since I moved there in 1975. 1 had seen the inevitable changes that growth inspires. Buried was that small college town in ever-enlarging, concentric circles of development, as though the Research Triangle Park had been a rock dropped in the middle of an arboreal pond. Raleigh, Durham, and Chapel Hill bound the edges once, but now the perimeter was creeping toward Hillsborough, Mebane, Cary, Pittsboro, and points east.

I had done my time in the government and academic institutions that, along with notable enclaves of private enterprise, fueled the engines of progress in the area. Having raised a family, punched someone else's clock for decades, studied the crafts of writing and acting, and yearned for a time and place to follow my Muse, I moved to Beaufort. Now a resident and no longer a tourist, the work of another lifetime showed promise for my access to an unfettered future.

II. The Creative Arts in Beaufort

When the senses first meet Beaufort and its intimate neighbor Port Royal, they are rewarded with a whiff of sea air and the sight of a grand, miniature downtown on the waterfront. Beaufort and Port Royal greet the eye as peaceful little towns on the South Carolina coast. But beneath that drowsy surface bubbles a ferment of artistic minds engaging the spiritual environment of greater Beaufort to create works of dramatic and literary art. Theater, creative writing, and dance thrive and grow.

The Beaufort Little Theater offers community theater productions several times each year. Smaller companies like the Rafael Sabatini Players, Rogues and Vagabonds, sponsored by the drama department at the University of South Carolina, Beaufort, Redbud Productions, and Wild Women Productions offer an eclectic mix of classical plays and new works by local playwrights.

The Byrne Miller Dance Theater and Beaufort Dance Company present both standard and new choreography.

The most popular venues for the local productions are The Shed Center for the Arts, and the auditoriums at the Battery Creek High School, the University of South Carolina at Beaufort, and the Technical College of the Low Country. Since losing our principal theater and company offering modern drama, Beaufort's performing arts community has shrunk somewhat in size, and been diminished in depth. We can only hope that it will be reborn here in the near future.

Beaufort is fortunate to be the home of the annual South Carolina Playwrights' Conference, a combination workshop and production company for the staged readings of original plays solicited throughout the eastern United States. I had the honor of serving as board member and Artistic Director of the 1997 Conference.

Many well-known writers such as Pat Conroy, Lois Battle, Sara Banks, and Charlotte Hughs call Beaufort home. Within Beaufort County, which includes Hilton Head Island, also live some of the finest poets in the Southeast, Dana Wildsmith and Fred Bassett to name two.

Beaufort nurtures its literary environment through annual workshops, Brewster Milton Robertson for fiction writing, and Dana Wildsmith for poetry.

The year 1998 focused national attention on Beaufort as a flower of the literary arts with the 2nd Annual Celebration of Writing in the Lowcountry. The conference boasted this year, as last, a plethora of events including eleven workshops led by nationally recognized writers in all aspects of the creation of poetry and fiction, including screenplays.

What a time-to live in Beaufort! Some persons move through life lamenting missed opportunity, believing themselves never to have been in quite the right place at quite the right time. That can be true, but on the other hand chance does, indeed, favor the mind that is prepared. Before Beaufort my mind was prepared but I often grimaced with an uneasy feeling that I somehow didn't fit my environment. Perhaps cosmic forces guide us, suggesting that destiny is not always under our complete control. Or call it luck, if you will. I have had the good fortune to find myself living in Beaufort where I belong. The creative arts community had a face and form before I arrived. When I found it I threw my arms around it and hugged with all my strength. It blossoms, and I am part of it. I cannot ask for more.

Katherine MacMurray 5th Grade

Hilton Head
Elementary

The Old Are Us

By Wilhelmina Mitchell

I gulped in the circling wind. Here was the house, sturdy, strong; But smaller than I remembered. It seems I could almost touch the roof. Sounds of laughter filled my thoughts. The aroma of good food cooking awoke my taste.

I asked aloud (how innocent of me), My heart and eyes aching to see, "Hey! Where is everyone?" Someone must be here! Only me?

Then I saw coming around the house, an elderly gent with cane in hand, jump up and say with a thrust, "Willie? Where have you been? Don't you know? Our folk are all gone. The old are us!"

Caryl Sweet

Comeyuh Come Home

By Natalie Daise

The Greyhound bus ride had taken about 24 hours, most of them uneventful if you don't count the wild-eyed man peering over the stalls in the women's restroom during the layover in Washington, DC. I re-read Scott O'Dell's children's classic, Island of the Blue Dolphins, because it seemed appropriate and tried to memorize Francis Thompson's poem, "The Hound of Heaven," in its entirety because I thought it might do me some good. The bus was heading for Florida. I was getting off in Beaufort, South Carolina. I had no expectations or knowledge of this place - just that the people here "talked funny and wore loud clothes," as reported by a relative who had visited once.

When the big gray dog crossed the invisible Mason-Dixon Line without incident (like the appearance of a horde of maniacal, hooded men with torches), I relaxed a little and looked out the dingy windows with some interest as I watched the landscape change. So this was "The South," that place of my parents' stories. I'd put in two weeks—three weeks tops—before I moved on to someplace else.

If you had asked why I was going to Beaufort, my response would have been that I was needed to help care for my sick Grandmother. That was true at the time, but it was also a convenient explanation. There is much that my explanation leaves out. It doesn't include, for instance, the suffocating weight of the man pushing me against the cold kitchen floor. It doesn't include the sound of my pleading that bounced, unanswered, off the ice-coated windows. It doesn't include the humiliations brought by the judicial system or the withdrawal of the religious community that had defined the boundaries of my life in the place I had called home. It tells nothing of the deep depression and fear that settled around me, making me incapable of leaving my house, opening the drapes, or answering the phone. There is nothing in the story of the sick grandmother that speaks of the effect that a stunned and disillusioned daughter, who never sleeps, has on her father's new marriage, or that I boarded the bus on the very day that my attacker began his sentence (plea-bargained to an easy few months), or that the ticket, bought for me by a relative, was only one-way. I said good-bye to no one. My grandmother's illness gave the journey an end. A destination. Gave purpose to what was, in fact, flight. I could have been going anywhere. The Greyhound bus that pulled into the cinder block station on Boundary St. on April 14, 1983 had rolled into town right down Ribaut Road

where the azaleas were doing their best to show off in every possible variation of pink. It was a striking contrast to the gray, sludge-edged puddles that herald spring in northwestern New York State.
The sun was shining. The air was damp and salty. I had, if not a sense of anticipation, at least a
sense of change. I entered the bus station lobby dragging one large suitcase and found a seat amidst
a group of young bald men. "We're the rejects," one informed me, "the ones the Marines don't
want." He laughed loudly and a few others joined in. I got the impression that none of them
thought it was really funny.

My Aunt picked me up about half an hour later. My father's baby sister, Willie Dee, had married
one of those Geechees years ago in Boston and he'd brought her back home. I didn't know them
well. Up until Uncle Simeon got the urge to "go home to his people," they had lived with their two
sons and my grandmother in Tucson, Arizona, so we only saw them once every few years or so. The
year that they had been back home had been a rough one. Their youngest son, my cousin Kevin,
died of misdiagnosed meningitis within months of their arrival, and my Grandmother, overcome
with grief, began to fail: first her spirits, then her kidneys. I was the runaway relief pitcher.

We didn't talk much on our ride to Grandma's. We passed over the Woods Memorial Bridge, visions
of O'Dell's blue dolphins swimming in my head, and then made a right turn behind the Red and
White Supermarket to a Ladies Island community known to locals as Hazel Farm. Grandma lived in
a little red and white striped trailer tied down behind a straight old pine tree with peeling bark. It
was located in the back yard of my uncle and aunt's house, a small, brick ranch style crammed with
foster boys, herbal remedies, grains bought in bulk, and books on natural healing and Bible apologetics.

Dull Spanish moss, looking like something out of a gothic movie, hung off the limbs of the old oak
trees surrounding the back yard. Strange insects were creating a racket. Inside, I had a small cubicle
with a cot (it was a tiny trailer). The little crank-operated window looked out on a wobbly wire
fence and an overgrown empty lot. I unpacked my suitcase into the open shelves along one wall of
my "room." The first night I lay on the cot, curled carefully on my left to avoid the large dip in the
center, and watched the largest roach I had ever seen make its way casually across the ceiling. When
it opened its wings and actually flew the rest of the way, I jumped up so fast my heart almost stut-
tered to a stop. I seriously considered re-packing my bag immediately and hopping the next bus out.
The few roaches I had encountered in my life up till then DID NOT FLY. It seemed, coupled with
their humongous size, an unfair advantage.

The second day into my first week in Hazel Farm, my aunt dropped me off downtown on her way
to work. Leaving me on the corner at the foot of the bridge, she said she'd pick me up at the end of

the day. I walked along Bay Street and in and out of the little stores that lined it. I bought some colored pencils and pens and a drawing pad. I ate ice cream. I sat in the swings on the waterfront and sketched pictures while I watched people and pets and boats go by. I didn't see any dolphins. But here is the strange thing. While walking through the Old Point I began to feel as though I was being watched. It was early afternoon. There were very few people about, and yet I felt it—that sensation one gets when one is the focus of unseen attention. I would glance suddenly over my shoulder, peering into the dark shadows under porches. I saw no one. But I couldn't shake the feeling—or the voice—that crept into my consciousness and would not leave: It's about time you got here, it said. What took you so long? Being the pragmatic fundamentalist I was, this was unnerving. But I wasn't frightened. I wondered who could have been waiting for me, and why.

Anthony Smalls, 10th Grade - Battery Creek High School

113

Getting to know my family brought its own wonders. My Uncle Simeon was a singularly optimistic man. He could not be convinced that Things wouldn't All Work Out For The Best and that the Love of God did not Conquer All. Seeing that he lived in a 3 bedroom ranch with 5 boys and his wife, had just lost his youngest son and was nursing an ailing mother-in-law, while working two jobs, growing a church, and trying to build an addition to the house by himself, this was some view. He held firmly to it. Frequently, after I'd gotten Grandmother tucked in for the night, he would walk across the dark yard to the trailer to sit up and talk until the wee hours of the morning. He always talked about the same thing. Love, he said, is what it's all about. God's love for us. Our love for Him. Our love for each other. That's what it's all about. It's the only lesson we have to learn. He was pretty dogmatic about it. Seeing that I was an insomniac and there was no TV, it didn't matter much to me what he had to say. I had nothing better to do. But I didn't believe him then.

Sometimes, when I'd walked across the yard to their house in the early evening he would tell stories of plat-eyes and hags and coach-whip snakes. I'd laugh during the telling, but walking back across that unlit acre of weeds later on, the blackness so dense I could feel it press against my skin, I would breathe quickly and quietly, watching from the corner of my eye for sudden movements– or unexplained sounds, of which there were always plenty.

When there was nothing I needed to do around the trailer or house, I'd ride sidekick with Simeon wherever he needed to go. We'd visit church or family members or other folk in the community who were ill and needed herbs, fresh carrot juice, enemas, or prayer. All of which he believed in strongly. Sometimes he would go get herbs from one of his sisters who lived in the Indian Hill community on St. Helena, and who collected the plants herself. One sister once told me that cayenne pepper tea cured painful cramps. After trying it, I was convinced. Pain is a relative thing. We occasionally rode out to Cornbread's place to see if there were any spare parts for one of Simeon's cars. My Uncle planned to consolidate the pieces of the many old cars scattered around his yard into one new car that worked. He believed in this, too. It was during one of these trips, the back of the aging van filled with lumber, spare parts, or produce, that my Uncle first said to me, "You know, you don't have to leave." It was coming up on my third week on the Island. I had never thought of staying. I didn't know where I would go when I left, just that I would. I didn't have a paying job. The future was a blank slate. "You don't have to leave," he said to me, "we take care of each other here."

Over the next couple of days, while caring for Grandmother and walking the dirt roads back off of Meridian Road, (Where I sometimes felt as though I'd stumbled into a rerun of "Sounder") I thought about the option he had offered me. The option to stay. To not run any farther. To find out who was waiting for me and why. Finally, I picked up the telephone in Grandma's trailer and used the rotary dial to call home. "Send my stuff," I told my Daddy, "I'm staying here for a while." We put in a garden that summer, my Aunt Dee and I. We tilled and planted and weeded and watered while Grandmother sat in the yard in an ugly vinyl kitchen chair and hollered orders: "Don't plant them peanuts so close together! Pull them little suckers off the corn or you won't get any good ears!" My feet, in the open sandals I wore, were baptized by fire ants and my arms and legs were spotted by scars made worse by my vigorous scratching. We harvested baskets of okra, several fat ears of corn, at least a bushel of peanuts and rows and rows of glossy green sweet potato vines, with nary a root beneath them big enough to cook. We were immensely proud. My Aunt and Uncle and cousins and I sat on the front porch in straight kitchen chairs eating watermelon and cantaloupe and waiting for the heat of the day to break. And I knew I was home.

It has been fifteen years since I came home. My friends up North think of me as a Southerner now. I've even been known to wear loud clothes and talk funny now and then. But around here, of course, I'm still a Comeyuh. Another hundred years here won't change that, despite that fact that I married one of those Geechees myself and have given birth to two children who are related to half the folk on St. Helena Island. But I am home nonetheless. I finally found out who had been waiting for me and why. It was about time I got here. There were stories to tell. And as I've told the stories I have discovered it was my voice that was waiting to be found in the cool shadowed places under porches and at peeling, blue-trimmed windows. My voice, moving with small suddenness in the velvet blackness of night; my voice, unclaimed, waiting to be given breath and song and heart, was waiting for me here. At home. And as my Uncle said, I don't have to leave.

Always move to Beaufort
If you love the water
Never move to Beaufort
If you don't have a daughter.

> Courtney McElveen, 3rd Grade
> Mossy Oaks Elementary

No Storms come to Beaufort and no tornadoes and no twisters and no tidal waves. I like the ocean because it is pretty. I like school. I like my friends. I like Beaufort.

> Mark Baird, 2nd Grade
> Shell Point Elementary

Oak Magic

By Stephen Gordin

Twenty-five years ago, my parents insisted on taking my brothers and me on a day trip to Beaufort, South Carolina. Although the distance was only eighty miles from our home in Summerton, it seemed like forever to three squirmy, complaining eight-to twelve-year olds.

"I wanted to go fishing today," I whined. "I don't want to walk around any old house."

Turning around from the front seat, my mother said, "But there's more to Beaufort than just old homes. They practice black magic and voodoo down there, you know."

"Really?"

"You'll see." She turned back around.

It was the right thing to say to a ten-year-old boy. I quieted as my imagination went into overdrive thinking about what we'd find in Beaufort. Would darkness hover over the trees? Would sorcerers and witches emerge from the mist and cast spells on the innocent? Would the old homes my parents talked so much about look like the old haunted house we had in Summerton?

At first, I was disappointed to find none of these things. It was a beautiful early spring day, and there was no misty gray hovering over the city. In fact, the area's many rivers reflected the sunlight so that the town seemed much brighter than any place I had ever been before. And, far from crumbling boards of an old farmhouse, Beaufort's old homes were solid, imposing structures with manicured lawns. There was no blackness to be found in town. Instead, the colors of their homes were like those of a French print we had in our house. ("That's pronounced Monay," my mother told me. "Not Mon-et.") They sported hues of soft pinks, soothing blues, and vivid lime greens. Their tones blended into one another, and I visualized Mr. Monay sitting on a riverbank, capturing Beaufort in its natural colors.

But what really caught my eye that day were the majestic oaks, the likes of which I had never seen. We saw them on the riverfront and in virtually every yard from the great mansions to the most modest dwellings. Along Beaufort's main street, their gnarled limbs stretched impressively to sometimes touch one another.

The Spanish moss that dripped from their branches hung gracefully in the light sea breezes and provided the only grayness I would see that day. I decided that if there were gnomes and other mystical creatures that lived in Beaufort, they must live in the sturdy trunks of these wonderful oaks. And, indeed, they must have, because pastel scenes of that day stuck in my mind like catfish spines and were just as impossible to remove. Through the years, those memories enchanted me, enticed me, and caused me to return to Beaufort over and over.

After my medical training, I was fortunate to find a practice in Beaufort. After moving here, I searched diligently for a home that would embody my romantic vision of this area. I wanted to be far away from the double-laned roads and fast-food chains, which were then just emerging. One day I drove down a dirt road, and I found my dream house. It was on a river, surrounded by woods and several great oaks, and painted in colors from Monet's palette. The many hundreds of undeveloped acres of land which surrounded the house at that time bestowed mystery and solitude upon it.

But that was a few years back.

Now, as Beaufort sprouts awkwardly like an adolescent, developers are clearing those woods to make room for others who have been enchanted by the Lowcountry's magic. I awake daily to the sounds of chainsaws, and when I return from work, I see the day's encroachment in the form of more sand and fewer trees. The underbrush is gone, as is the wildlife that used to call it home. Smaller oaks have been cut down without regard to the mystical creatures residing within them. An asphalt road suddenly appears through the remaining trees. As I sadly observe this carnage, I wonder how much longer the original spell cast upon me can endure.

Brian Ashley, 10th Grade - Hilton Head High

But my attitude changed last Sunday when my son John and I walked down the newly cut road, which leads to the river's marshes. I had begun our walk with my mood matching the darker gray colors of an overcast day. And yet, my emotional hues changed when I reached the water. We were able to see that the developers had left more trees there than were visible from our house. The smaller trees encircled and seemed to pay homage to a massive oak. Its branches reached over the water and back to the land and seemed to jealously guard the nature under its charge.

"Wow!" 5-year old John exclaimed. "That sure is a big tree!"

"It sure is," I agreed. "It must be a thousand years old." Apparently, I was not alone in my belief about the importance of the great oaks. I decided that these developers knew they had left more than just a tree; they had reasserted the belief that the Lowcountry's uniqueness is more important than unrestrained growth. They had saved more than a tree; they had momentarily saved the haunting spirit of Beaufort. Change is coming to this part of the South, but it is not necessarily something to fear as long as the area's romanticism endures. I suddenly realized that I am a part of the cycle myself; yes, I am a part of that change because it was this magic that summoned me here. My son and I stood watching the river through the oak's branches until peaks of sunlight began emerging through the gray clouds and reflected off the water. Suddenly, the atmosphere was much brighter.

"You know," I said, crouching down and putting my arm around my son. "They practice magic down here in the Lowcountry..."

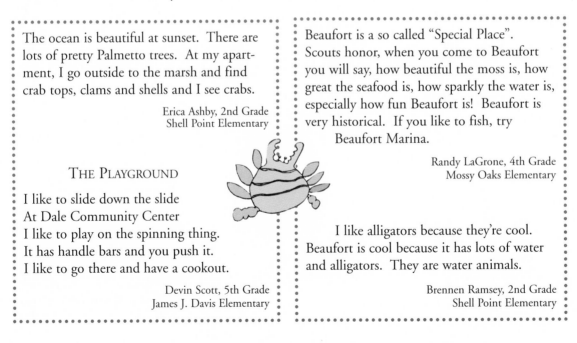

The ocean is beautiful at sunset. There are lots of pretty Palmetto trees. At my apartment, I go outside to the marsh and find crab tops, clams and shells and I see crabs.

Erica Ashby, 2nd Grade
Shell Point Elementary

THE PLAYGROUND

I like to slide down the slide
At Dale Community Center
I like to play on the spinning thing.
It has handle bars and you push it.
I like to go there and have a cookout.

Devin Scott, 5th Grade
James J. Davis Elementary

Beaufort is a so called "Special Place". Scouts honor, when you come to Beaufort you will say, how beautiful the moss is, how great the seafood is, how sparkly the water is, especially how fun Beaufort is! Beaufort is very historical. If you like to fish, try Beaufort Marina.

Randy LaGrone, 4th Grade
Mossy Oaks Elementary

I like alligators because they're cool. Beaufort is cool because it has lots of water and alligators. They are water animals.

Brennen Ramsey, 2nd Grade
Shell Point Elementary

Dan Brown

Beaufort County Library

The Beaufort County Library is the biggest Library in Beaufort. The library has two sections. The sections are the Adult Section which has adult books, and the other section is the Children and teenage section which has those kind of books. To check out a book you have to have a library card. If you are a child when you get your library card you can't get another card until you are 15. You have to whisper in the library. In the children's and teenager section they have a thing that you put the amount of the books and if you read them you get a free book.

Cherelle Patterson, 4th Grade
Mossy Oaks Elementary

Rock-Bottom on Hilton Head Island

By Patricia Deaton

No one starts out to be an addict. It just happens. Perhaps it is because of the way one is brought up. Who knows? All I know is I have an overwhelming desire for items which have had a previous life. No brand-spanking-new retail purchases for me. Give me shirts that have seen it all, shoes that have hopped to a forgotten tune and furniture with family secrets hidden under cushions and tucked inside drawers.

Thrift shop addiction knows no class, color, or ethnic origin. We are legion. Look around.

Are you sure that lady in the Escada blouse paid full retail price or did she get it for a fraction of the original cost? Comment on her blouse. If she got it for a song, she'll tell you, eyes aglitter, where to go...for a bargain, of course. On Hilton Head Island, the source is the Bargain Box.

Billie Hack, Irene Wilkins, and Mary Alice Williamson started the charitable resale phenomenon in 1965 in an unheated cinder-block building with no running water. In 1981, the Bargain Box moved to its present location. For seventeen years, junk-store junkies have nursed their habit in the red brick building that sits at the back of the First Presbyterian Church property on Highway 278.

A few hitch-hike to get there, some drive BMW's, others arrive on bicycles, but they all come for the same reason. Pianos to pin cushions, surfboards to sombreros, wallets to washing machines. There is something to satisfy everyone's craving...at rock-bottom prices.

On Saturday mornings, Monday, Wednesday, or Friday afternoons, a line forms at the front steps of the store. The first hundred people in line receive numbered tickets, entitling the holders to first crack at the treasures when the doors open.

On a certain Friday, visions of bargains dancing in my head drive me to the Bargain Box. When I arrive, a volunteer is out front, tearing tickets from a roll. He hands me #46. I smugly pocket the ticket and look around me.

Young mothers, blue-collar workers, elderly on fixed incomes, professional people, and preppy-looking caddies from the local golf courses come, along with out-of-towners who head here first when they cross the bridge.

Listening to conversations spoken with accents as diverse as vehicles in the parking lot breaks up the monotony of waiting. Rapid-fire Spanish ricochets off the pine trees. Eclectically dressed youths stand nonchalantly.

A few early-comers bring folding chairs to sit and eat fast food or read the newspaper or a paperback while they wait. Others grab their tickets and rush off to do errands, or (if it's Saturday morning) to check out nearby yard sales, then return minutes before time to go in. Most are in a good mood. Who would guess we are addicts, waiting for a "fix"?

I walk around the building and finagle my way through the back entrance. Inside the Bargain Box, no one is standing around. About thirty of the three-hundred-plus volunteers, as well as four paid-employees and an office manager, are busy preparing for the onslaught of people, crazy for a bargain.

To date, no effort has been made to quell the rampancy of thrift shop addiction in the Low Country. As a result, revenues from the Bargain Box are responsible for a recent gift of 250,000 dollars to help build the Boys and Girls Club on Hilton Head. Scholarships have been established over the years. Deep Well and The Children's Center are just two of the many charities in Beaufort County receiving seventy-five percent of the Bargain Box profits. No one really likes to talk about money, though.

Evelyn, in collectibles, who holds the record for twenty-seven years of volunteering, talks about the great time she has helping out. Fellowship is her most valuable "find" at the Bargain Box.

"I'm here on Fridays and we have a potluck lunch on the 4th Friday of every month. It's so much fun," she says.

"Of course, everyone thinks "their" day is more fun than any other," laughs Bargain Box president Betsy Catlin as she places a garbage bag at the foot of "Mount Charity" — a huge pile of dark green garbage bags full of clothing, waiting to be sorted, inspected, priced, and hung.

The benevolent spirit of the three remarkable women who started the Bargain Box shines on the faces of the volunteers as books, toys, sports equipment, housewares ...just about anything one could imagine, is made ready for the crowd lining up out front.

A woman who lost everything when her rented moving van was stolen walks through the work areas, selecting items courtesy of the Bargain Box to help restock her household and renew her spirit.

A few other customers are in the store, even though the doors aren't open yet. Senior and mentally retarded citizens are allowed to shop early so they don't have to contend with the crowd. Kindness abounds at the Bargain Box.

Leah, the bright-eyed "head of volunteer" is keeping up with ten such shoppers who have come from Hardeeville. While she bustles around helping with their purchases, she informs me that volunteers who work at least three hours a week, get "first pick" of fifteen dollars worth of items. I volunteer.

It's almost time for the doors to open. Taking one last look around at this incredible recycling operation, I head out the back door. A woman is dropping off a couple of bags of donations. She says she'll probably go inside and buy two more bags full of "stuff". We shake our heads and laugh. I think about the life of an item donated to the Bargain Box; the journey, from the time it ends up on the receiving dock at the back entrance until the time it goes out the front door, home with its new owner...and beyond. I see the larger picture; one hand extended, another taking hold, a perfect circle of giving.

As I walk around the building to take my place in line, I pat the pocket holding my ticket. A volunteer's voice, first in English, then in Spanish, comes over the loudspeaker, welcoming everyone to the Bargain Box. At the front steps, a taxi pulls up. A disheveled-looking man with a two-day old beard gets out and tries to buck the line.

I should give him my ticket. After all, I really don't need a thing and besides, didn't I just volunteer?

I flip the ticket nervously against my thumb, trying to decide what to do. The craving is back, stronger than ever, pulling me like a giant magnet. I think to myself, I can kick this habit. The

doors open up. A volunteer begins to collect the tickets. The line lurches forward. I double-check my number. A hand reaches for my ticket. I give it up.

Suddenly, I am inside, and out of control. I grab a plastic shopping basket and rush past old record albums, rows of clothes and tables of shoes and sweaters. I head to the furniture department even though my apartment is so crowded I can't fit in another thing.I see a lamp I have to have, and a picture, and a little chest I stand guard over until someone can come put a "Sold" tag on it for me. My head is reeling. I buy a half-price coffee maker, even

Sophie Nichols, 4th Grade - Broad River Elementary

123

though I have a perfectly good one at home. . . and knitting needles for ten-cents apiece. I have never knitted in my life. . . but I might.

A Bleyle jacket is just old enough to be "funky" and I snap it up for $7. Next, I fish a ring out of a box of assorted ones marked "one dollar each" and ask for the magnifying glass kept behind the counter for inspections. When I peer through the glass at the enlarged image of the ring, I feel like one of the dealers who come with their "loops" to examine items in the collectibles case, except I don't know what I'm looking for.

"I'll just wear it," I say and shove the ring onto my finger, then hand over a dollar and silently vow to try and cut glass with the stone when I get home.

A hot-pink cap with the word "Sail" written on it calls to me from a shelf near the front checkout. I stuff it in my overloaded basket.

As I wait in line to pay, I collect my thoughts, breathing deeply and evenly. For a second, I see myself putting everything back where I found it, secure in the fact that, for once, I have not succumbed to my urges. Nahhhh. If I get home and don't have room for everything, I can always call the Bargain Box to come pick up whatever I need to get rid of.

I have a problem. Remember? You know how the saying goes. Once an addict. . .

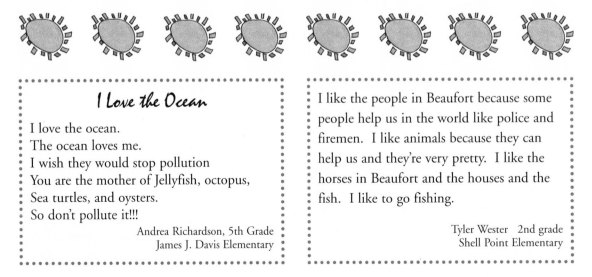

I Love the Ocean

I love the ocean.
The ocean loves me.
I wish they would stop pollution
You are the mother of Jellyfish, octopus,
Sea turtles, and oysters.
So don't pollute it!!!

Andrea Richardson, 5th Grade
James J. Davis Elementary

I like the people in Beaufort because some people help us in the world like police and firemen. I like animals because they can help us and they're very pretty. I like the horses in Beaufort and the houses and the fish. I like to go fishing.

Tyler Wester 2nd grade
Shell Point Elementary

Rebecca Davenport - "No Bill" 1992

901 Bay Street

By Nancy Ricker Rhett

901 Bay Street was probably built in 1879. A Union Officer purchased the land at a tax sale in 1865, but there is no record of a structure on the land. In 1889, there was a Chinese laundry downstairs, then Dr. Stuart had his dentistry there. My aunt, who died at age 92, said that as a girl, the Ribault Club held meetings upstairs at 901 Bay Street, and she went to dances up there. Early in the Twentieth Century, the building was used for a dry goods store, and upstairs rooms were partitioned off to provide a residence for the storekeepers.

In about 1926 the dry goods store was replaced by Hirsch's Shoe Store. When we moved into the store we found piles and piles of old records dating back to 1926. Each year's receipts were kept in neat little stacks. The earliest receipts were tied with string. Later receipts sported dried out rubber bands. Paper clips held the next crop of receipts and the most recent receipts were stapled. It was an interesting history lesson. Everything was carefully saved. When the shelves were full, new shelves were added in front of or above the old ones. It was a maze of shelving in the storage area. The long wooden counters in the front room had hundreds of little crescent-shaped dents. Apparently, they only displayed one shoe and it hung on a shoebox on the shelves. To hang the shoe the clerk put a carpenter's tack into the heel of it, then banged the heel against the counter top to drive the tack in resulting in about 75 years worth of dents.

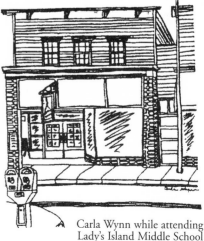

Old Mrs. Rosenthal came to look around and told us that she had worked there when she was young. She pointed to a place on the counter. "That," she said, "is where I kept the jar of alcohol." She went on to tell us that in the 1920's, women who worked at the oyster factory across the river rowed to town in their bateaux to shop. Their clothes, probably crocus sacks, had no pockets so they stored their nickels and dimes in their cheeks, like chipmunks. To make a purchase, they spit their money into the jar of alcohol. Mrs. Rosenthal said the constant dipping into the alcohol for the money made her hands so chapped she had to keep a supply of lotion handy.

Carla Wynn while attending
Lady's Island Middle School

Writing in Beaufort Cafes

By Michael Haynes

It's said if you stay in one place long enough, you'll see the world eventually pass by you. I've never been one to remain that long in any place myself, preferring instead to see the world before it gets the chance to see me. But the life I've made for myself, and where I've chosen to live that life, has given the world and me the opportunity to continually cross paths. You see, I write in cafes. That means while the rest of you come into one for a mocha latte or gossip or a chance to catch your breath between golf and touring, I'm actually working there, even if I'm rarely paid for it.

I've written in cafes since I was sixteen years old - first in the college hangouts of New Jersey where I could pass myself off as a student and not get thrown out - later in places from Boston to Berlin to New Orleans. I was thrown out of some regardless of my age. Now I'm writing in Beaufort, half-a-lifetime later, on the first truly cool day of autumn here, with the leaves of the trees at the Firehouse Books & Espresso Bar showering my table. I've done fine work in the time that I've written at this place, and at others in town and around the county. I've made friends and enemies, and seen the tourist buggies pass by here on Craven Street a thousand times. Here comes another - the horse is pulling a full carriage and once again a little part of the world and I meet.

In fact, that was how I first found this place. I was on vacation and it was my first time in the Lowcountry so, just like everyone else, I took the carriage tour. As it passed by this picturesque brick building with its little piazza, I saw three cyclists at a table, but, more importantly, also saw two empty tables and knew I'd have to write there. So I went home, quit my job in the music business, sold my possessions, said good-bye to the landlord and good riddance to the two rotten cats that ran my rented house. A month later I was sitting at that same table where the cyclists had sat, finishing my first novel. That was two years, two books and two literary agents ago. I think it was the best choice I ever made; you would also, especially after living with those rotten cats.

I can't claim to have written in all the cafes throughout Beaufort County, and this essay is in no way intended as a guide or review of them for those seeking to follow the anachronistic way in which I pursue my profession. It's not my intent to tell you how I've felt or fared while writing at them either. Though writing is the largest form of communication, its creation is still a mystery, even to those who practice it. The closest I could come to describing it would be to describe the sunlight as its falls through the Spanish moss on Craven Street two hours before dark — or watching from the porch of Plum's, the Woods Memorial Bridge turning on its axis to let a sailboat pass — or listening to the different music filtering from the shops and restaurants into Java Joe's on Hilton Head. But that wouldn't tell you all about writing in cafes - it'd only be a start.

In the end, though, these are only places - locations, tables, coffee cups and ashtrays and pleasant weather, if you're lucky. It's the people you encounter in a cafe which truly makes the place what it is - the staff and owners, the regular customers, the visitors. It's what gives any place in any city or region its individuality, and it's what makes Beaufort more unique than any other area where I've lived and written.

Beaufort is a colony. I don't mean that in terms of its gated communities, its recreational resources or its tendency to draw artists and golfers to itself. I mean an old-style, emigrant colony, where people have come from all over the country and world to start anew, to stake personal claims, to make new lives. Most of the people I know are not from here; I didn't choose it that way; that's just how it is. This emigration has been so recent, too, that a distinct culture among the newcomers has

yet to emerge, and probably won't for at least another generation. Just like the first settlers centuries ago, they've brought their original stories and ways here with them. Of course, the indigenous cultures - the Gullah, the Old South - are still prevalent, and you don't have to travel far to find them, but so far neither the old nor new has fully blended into something cohesive. They haven't gelled into a distinct culture that can be labeled and defined as belonging exclusively to this region. This is a place of a potential culture, not a realized one.

It's a fascinating time to be here. No place else have I been with people and heard stories from the West, or Europe,

Carla Wynn while attending
Lady's Island Middle School

129

or right here in Beaufort County, all in one sitting. In any other place, the people would be too hesitant to share them, too apprehensive to appear like foreigners or make fools of themselves by opening their mouths. It can't be done in New York, or Paris, or any other place in The South. Having spent a quarter of my life here, I can write with experience in that particular matter. Beaufort permits this, encourages it, and although stories have always been my currency, I don't believe the advantage is solely mine. To tell the truth, I don't go to cafes to write anyone else's stories - I will listen to any that is told but, frankly, I've got enough of my own to keep me busy.

Still, there's plenty I've heard and liked, heard and regretted as well. I won't gloss it over - though I have the greatest friends here, I've also met my share of liars, cheats and morons in Beaufort. Overall, however, it's been better than worse, which is more than I can say of other places I've chosen to live. Sometimes, too, I've gotten help with one of my stories, like the time my dear friend Arianne at La Sirena inadvertently gave me the philosophical core of my second book. I'm not going to explain how that happened; I've told her twice and it's still a mystery to her. And I never know when surprises are in store either, such as when Jay Leno rushed into the Authors Bookstore Cafe desperately seeking a bathroom, or A Clockwork Orange star Malcolm McDowell scowled at me outside the Firehouse. That was a particular honor for me, even if no one else seemed to know who he was. That never happened at Cafe Voltaire on The Left Bank.

Two years isn't that long to get to know a place, but already I've seen the changes. Authors on Hilton Head sold off their large, beautiful cafe-portion of the store, which is now a pub. La Sirena is no more either; they even got rid of the wrought-iron patio furniture I loved to write on so much. On the other hand, the new Barnes & Noble on Hilton Head is turning into a great place to work late at night when the impulse seizes me. No doubt other changes to my favorite places are in store for the future. I hope whatever those changes are that they'll balance themselves out in time.

It's not just writers who need a clean, well-lighted cafe to gather. It's all of us - the natives, the new-comers, and the visitors - who need them, to meet, to gather, to gossip and to learn of one another. Where else can that happen? Bars are for drinking, clubs are for dancing, and restaurants are for eating. However fine they are, and no matter how much fun you have in them, they don't have the same purpose as a cafe. They're not supposed to be that way. Only in cafes will you find a certain kind of camaraderie, the meeting of different people from different worlds and, if for just the time it takes to drink a cup of coffee, a blending of those people into something new.

I can feel those falling leaves striking my head. Another carriage comes up Craven Street, and the guide is again telling of the 1907 fire started by two boys smoking. I hope there's always a place like this. ♣

Letty Lee Saville

Will Cook

The Graduate

Sherman's tracks are covered
by sweetblown Confederate Jasmine.
Stepping out in a Charleston carriage
driven by a grown-wild Citadel child
   (imagine, this boy once cropped into cadet)—
   long hair now drawn back but not held quite;
   ponytail unbranded, not like the horse
   who, southern to the core, pulls away
   from the right curb any chance he gets—
tendrils of the South curling on tabby walls
as Chad chants his rhythm of the past
at stucco and old wrought iron rails
—graveyards where war feeds blossom—
proving in the present that you can lead
a child to slaughter, but you can't make him
synchronize his patter with the canter of regret.

Sheila Tombe

Nancy Ricker Rhett

Jet Encounter

Jets runway bound
Thunder their presence across blue sky
White clouds bounce along
Behind stark black wings of might.

Crows crouch on perches
Anchored in the rising tide
Beaks pointed to the wind
Feathers raised in anticipated flight

Jets arch 'round salt-sprinkled marsh
And disappear on runways
Hidden on a hot July afternoon.

I rock by in their noise-wake
And try to name my uneasy fear.
Comforted by cushions warmed by the
Summer sun
I try to convince myself that all
Is well.

I sail around Coosaw bend
And sight the next mark

The jets and I leave each other behind.
The tide turns
I hike out
Giving balance to my small craft.

Melba Cooper

Dan Brown

Marine Corps Housing

On Parris Island, the unmarried are folded
into tiny apartments with toy kitchenettes.
These officers' quarters are called an inn
— The Osprey — an appropriate name
for loners who spend time circling the nest,
antiseptic bachelors supplied with hotel soaps
and clean white towels. The place is institutional
in strategic lines; concrete blocks breathe
the same air over;
outside, marshland meets the river
and the boat basin rinses clear.

Now. Imagine the Lt. Col. married, say, with three kids.
Instant promotion: from in-patient to head of household.
That easy. Well-appointed home
("they knew how to build in those days")
with a screened porch for the evenings,
where he stands, glass of wine in hand,
while the children squabble over homework,
the wife opens windows to catch the breeze,
and the osprey flies to its nest on headland,
bulwarked from the rising river
by the steep-banked channel in the mud.

Sheila Tombe

Penny Russell

Dan Brown

Sacrificial Fox

(Elegy to a Dead Fox Beside the Road Just Outside a Development Project That is
"Conducive to the Feeling of Being at One with Nature")

Limp fox lying in the ribbon grass
Across from that mud rutted road
Slash-routed by tons of yellow grinding.
Not stiff or bloody or mangled.
Just rust and quicksilver,
Outstretched toward the sleep of death.

If I but knew the words
To call you back
I would say them.
But they would be magic words,
And I know no magic.

Or is it that you chose this?
Chose not to struggle with
The claws that come at you now?
That gouge out your den
for sand traps and septic tanks.
Backhoe. Dragline. Bulldozer.
They are death.

How do you fight a dead enemy?
How do you fight any enemy?
You become like him.
You die.

Memory is the last refusal.
And now you have taken yours —
Wild and stealthy remembrances —
And gone away
From this heedless place,
Where reason withers with the sounds
Of saws and hammers, and the insistent
Pbfeep, Pbfeep, Pbfeep of heavy equipment backing up.

Later, when your bones are bleached,
They will mark the fringe of woodlands
Once untrammeled
Where freedom lay on the cusp one day,
Waiting for an answer.

But for now, As they strip your bright flesh hindward,
The dump truck driver can watch the vultures
Hop and flap around you in the rear view mirror
As he bounces down his hacked out road to paradise.

Ellen Malphrus

For One Thing

Not write of shrimpboats again, either,
but leave their whiteness to paint
and the ocean's blue to weather's wiles -
eye being slower than lettering hand

to tell buoy from boat, boat from breaker,
distinguish the funnel of a waterspout
from a billowing helix of birds
swirling out of the river's mouth,

nor how two sharks, come idling,
in synchrony a slick between low
swells, are but the gray wingtips
of a devil ray riding the slough

like a sledding cow, the ocean slack
over the broad shallows of its back.

Charles H. Ash

Lynn McLaren - *Ebb Tide–Flood Tide*

Afternoon Sea Breeze

The afternoon sea breeze continues with
the night and all that it brings.

A host of many may come.

Darkness, apparitions, and voids in our
senses which recoil when deprived,
The new moon comes out the back door
silent and hidden.

Her powers of persuasion are keenly
sharpened on the edges of fine celestial
positioning and she bids her sisters the
tides to rise.

Incoming, incoming, incoming rise, rise,
rise

higher, higher, higher
and with the silent rush and the brush
of a paddle's thrust
a myriad more coastal visions appear
sweating off the unseen necks
of terrestrials hidden by the night.

Out of the west, big tubs of rust are
drinking oils and bobbing with the
pulsing of the sea.

Its lights anxiously scan the Loran grid in
search of something, anything, while
thousands of creatures scurry by
unnoticed

Scott Gordon

Eric Horan

The Wave of the Future

"Well it's the wave of the future,"
　　Says the old, black minister,
　　his serene gaze reflecting
　　the glow of a room full of
　computer screens.
His grip tightens and the lines in
　　his hand tell stories of a day
　　when the wave was always
　　offshore,
　　a safe distance barely
　out of sight.
Then, technology was bound mainly
　　to the same hand before the
　　onslaught of culture and anarchy
　　pulsating in a steady
　stream of light.

10001110110011110100100011110101

The waves begin to crash and
　　fingers clamor
　　for the sand receding
　　into the rush of
　water.
The sun disappears into a
　　green orb of brine
and
　　as the last breath is drawn,
　　it becomes apparent that
there is no past,
there is no future,　　only
the ceaseless throb of swells
defining the present.

Scott Gordon

Joan Templer

Space in Effect - John Sumner, 10th Grade - Beaufort High School

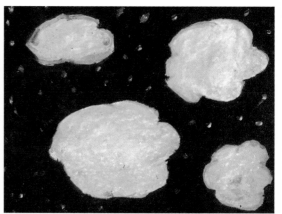

Clouds in Space - Paul Kearns 10th Grade, - Beaufort High School

River Sign - Andrea Nidess, 10th Grade - Beaufort High School

Geoscape - Geny Hatfield, 10th Grade - Beaufort High School

The Magic Bus

By Gabrielle Baggette Watson

We had started the '89 school year and I had just moved to Beaufort from Washington, DC. I had met Steve Wylie and Keith Walters through some of our Art classes and we hung out a lot at school and after. One Saturday, we were perusing some junk store and spotted a beat up, old Volkswagon bus. I am not sure who threw out some ideas about what we could do with it, but we were on a roll in minutes. It was a hundred dollars and I wrote my very first check to buy it. I think somebody's dad towed it to my house, where we attacked it with spray paint. Keith found some specialty Volkswagon magazine, which we all pored over in class. I can not remember who came up with the idea between Caroline Goforth (creative writing) & Melba Cooper (art teacher), but somehow the bus was adopted by the school and became the symbol for our literary magazine. So, now we had a creative writing class that we could talk about it everyday and it was now located in the school's shop so we could actually doodle on it everyday. We asked for submissions for the magazine, from poetry to art, and had all kinds of fun drives. I remember making vests for people out of paper bags for some reason or another. The crazy spray paint job we had initially done had disappeared under a whole new coat of paint. That van grew eyes and and waves and lots of little details. Keith got hold of a video camera and even shot a documentary video. We had a lot of fun doing it but I could not tell you what happened to that bus. Last I heard it got towed out to Lady's Island after the school year. The magazine was very successful and I think the bus generated a lot more interest in the magazine than we thought. We had a lot of help from people outside of our class and it was something that the school could watch it change everyday. I think Keith might know the final resting place of the bus, but we have not been in touch for years.

Sketch of Magic Bus by Keith Walters while attending Beaufort High School

Kenneth Robinson, 11th Grade - Beaufort High School "Ace Gateway"

Back To The Garden

By Jacki Martin

Our canoe, having traveled down river for some six or seven miles, drifts now, in a post-picnic reverie. We are moving through the Combahee River's plantation stretch; lush forested shoreline, gleaming dark water, a profoundly blue sky arching overhead. We have met an alligator –my first– and a wildlife officer, young, tanned, diffident. All parties sunwarmed, content, unhurried. Lunch was an illicit picnic, pulled up on a wildflowered shore not public, and perhaps for that reason irresistible. Now we nose past a great osprey's nest, the mother circling, noisily guarding her twigged and moss draped home. I see a large black bird and squint at it, then note the unmistakable white head of the American bald eagle.

This Combahee is one of three sweet rivers that form the renowned ACE Basin, our Lowcountry "wetland wilderness." The rivers –Ashepoo, Combahee, Edisto– course through the ACE's 350,000 acres of wetland, upland and forest, spilling over parts of Beaufort, Colleton, Charleston and Hampton counties. The ACE Basin is a rare jewel of a wetland system, largely intact and in many parts near pristine. Myriad species of wildlife and plantlife are birthed, sheltered, and fed on this land; its undefiled natural communities are sought-after real estate for animals abandoning other, corrupted systems. From the ACE Basin comes the stuff of traditional Lowcountry life, from the aesthetic values of its sights and sounds to the fishes, oysters, shrimp, deer and other animals that have long filled Lowcountry plates.

I have spent some time on the ACE rivers, and their beaches, swamps, forests, hidey-holes. Little sister Ashepoo, winding dark and gentle over the land; beautiful, storied Combahee; and the Edisto, as nice a stretch of blackwater as ever you'll see. So much I've seen. A midnight moonlit paddle in a silvery cypress swamp, eerie and other-worldly. An October boatride, surreal in the achingly blue sky, old-gold spartina, and complete absence of other humans. A still-wild beach washed with a thin mirror of water, reflecting a sunset panorama of blue sky, white clouds, pink and gold light. A spiky tangle of spider lilies fringing a creek, a limestone bluff cum hanging garden, a hidden rookery of improbable woodstorks. So much I've seen– and so little. So much more there.

The ACE Basin, says The Nature Conservancy, is one of the last great places. Indeed, so fine, so rare, that a coalition of private and public partners have abandoned distrust and competing agendas and territorial instincts and woven a tapestry of innovative protection measures for 128,000 of these acres– and counting. 128,000 acres of our fragile rich rare legacy that will not fall to the implacable, insatiable and indiscriminate bulldozer that is the mascot of the ubiquitous development by devastation team.

No being with any remnant of soul can enter the surfeit splendor of the ACE and remain unchanged. These places have had no less profound an effect on me than to cause me to reconsider both God and man. Here my long-skeptical soul can no longer deny the Creator, more present to me than ever in any human-built church. And the protective acts of people to save this land lend me the beginning of hope that perhaps our sense of what is good and proper and necessary may overcome our greed and foolishness; that we might yet attain the evolutionary destiny assigned us by an optimistic God. Might yet become the keepers of this Garden.

And back on the Combahee, on a spring afternoon in an idling canoe, I look back at my paddling partner, he an ecologist, an activist, a man of great passion for the land and anger toward its enemies, but he does not see me; his face is calm and like a small boy's, lifted to the sun. And in that moment –in *that* moment– I am becalmed and bequieted and touched with Grace.

And all of a piece, we drift on.

Will Cook

Dan Brown

Melody Brown while attending Beaufort High School

A Personal Perspective

WHERE IS - WHAT IS THE ESSENCE OF BEAUFORT?

The Essence of Beaufort resides in the hearts and souls of its people and it may never completely be defined. Each of us looks out from a different window. Each of us sees a different facet of this gem we call Beaufort County.

The remaining pages of this book are set aside for the reader to add his or her own perspective. Think about all the things Beaufort and the Lowcountry mean or have meant to you. Look around you and define what is special and worthy of remembering. What do you want to pass on to future generations? What is it about Beaufort County that you want to keep forever?

Hope Jenkins, 5th Grade - St. Helena Elementary

Maybe you like to sketch or draw, or to collect and press wild flowers. Maybe taking snapshots appeals to you. A thought, a memory, a little poem or a special story is begging to be written down. Your families, your friends, and your memories are all important. They are part of your viewpoint and therefore a valid part of the Essence of Beaufort.

If you live outside of Beaufort County and have been a visitor here, you may recall a special experience or something about Beaufort County that stands out for you.

Perhaps one day we can gather together and share what we have put in our last pages and another book will be born.

153

Shedreka Perry, 5th Grade - St. Helena Elementary

Raenell Robinson, 4th Grade - St. Helena Elementary

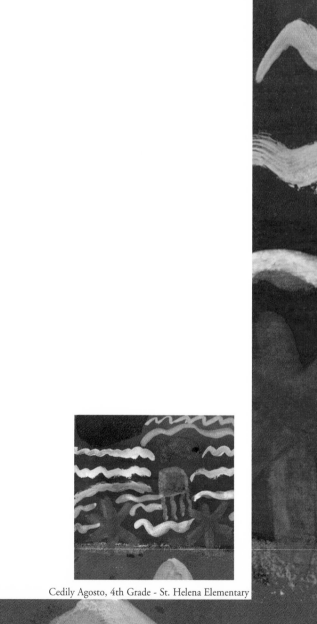

Cedily Agosto, 4th Grade - St. Helena Elementary

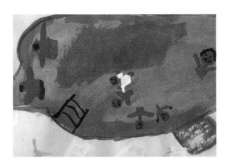

Ashley Gordon, 5th Grade - St. Helena Elementary

Christina Williams, 3rd Grade - St. Helena Elementary

Terry Jenkins, 3rd Grade - St. Helena Elementary

Tacara Boles, 5th Grade - St. Helena Elementary

Quinton Smalls, 3rd Grade - St. Helena Elementary

Barrett Menning, 4th Grade - St. Helena Elementary

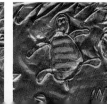

Shedreka Perry, 5th Grade - St. Helena Elementary

Demetria White, 5th Grade - St. Helena Elementary

In Conclusion

Waukeria Birch, 5th Grade - St. Helena Elementary

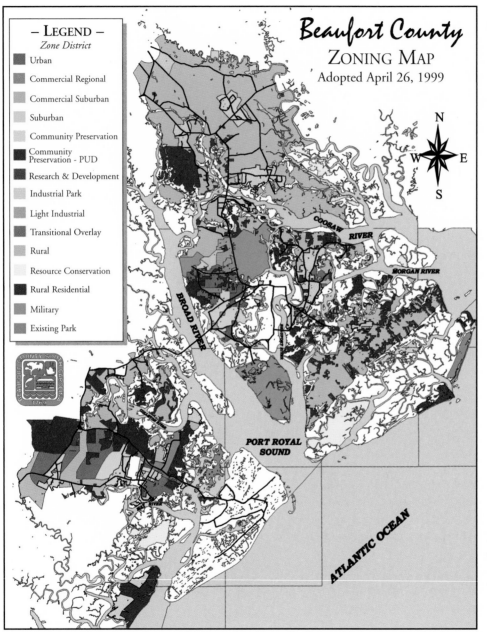

- LEGEND -
Zone District

Urban
Commercial Regional
Commercial Suburban
Suburban
Community Preservation
Community Preservation - PUD
Research & Development
Industrial Park
Light Industrial
Transitional Overlay
Rural
Resource Conservation
Rural Residential
Military
Existing Park

Beaufort County
ZONING MAP
Adopted April 26, 1999

N
W E
S

COOSAW RIVER
MORGAN RIVER
BROAD RIVER
PORT ROYAL SOUND
ATLANTIC OCEAN

Prepared by Beaufort County GIS Department

Contributing Artists and Writers

Joe Adams, a writer for over 45 years, is a resident of Hilton Head Island. He is an award winning playwright and essayist and a regular contributor to the international art magazine, Raw Vision. His humorous essays appear in regional and national magazines.

Charles H. Ash's poems are full of love for the marsh, the sea, and for poetry. Chick was a valued, honest, and generous friend. He volunteered much of his time as a handyman at Penn Center and, when he wasn't wielding a hammer, he was writing about the Low Country and the people he met here. Chick died on Oct 8, 1998.

Sandra Baggette is an award winning full-time artist who has exhibited in over 100 juried shows from Maryland to Florida. She is an active member of several watercolor societies and is a founding board member of the Arts Council of Beaufort County. She developed her Garden Studio Gallery in Port Royal, SC in1988.

Dan Brown is a native Carolinian who has taught art in Beaufort for twenty years. He earned a BA in art from Fuhrman University and a BFA from Clemson in Painting. His art reflects his love for the Lowcountry.

Carolyn Enloe Bremer is a Native Alabaman who has lived with her husband in Bluffton since 1983. She graduated from Rosemont

College in PA and did graduate work at USCB. She has taught, is a Real Estate Broker, and for the past several years has written her "Beautiful Bluffton" column for local papers.

Hildred Fern Collier has lived in Beaufort for 45 years and has watched it change from a sleepy seaside town to a metropolis. She says: "I loved all the people and the trees and now the old people and the old trees are going away."

Will Cook is a graduate of the Savannah College of Art and Design and is a commercial photographer in Beaufort. In recent years, he has focused on aerial photography.

Melba Cooper teaches art at Beaufort High School and was named Secondary Educator of the year in 1992. She established Frogmore Pottery at Coffin Point after which she co-founded the Craftseller. The Low Country has inspired her work since 1975.

Natalie Daise, a transplanted New Yorker, shares with her husband, Ron: two wacky children, a house on the water, a television and theatre career, a huge extended family, and a deep belief in the Grace of God. She knows that "Gullah Gullah Island" is a fantasy world but believes that love, respect, appreciation, and a liberal dose of music enrich any community, real or imagined.

Gloria Dalvini was trained in graphic design at Kendall College of Art and Design in Michigan. For many years she free-lanced in her own design business. She now devotes full time to watercolor painting in her studios in Beaufort, SC and Holland MI. Beaufort and the Low Country are the subjects of her paintings, which are on view at her studio at 101 Scott Street.

Rebecca Davenport says, "Art is about communication. It expands the mind opening our eyes to how we view our environment and ourselves. My latest works are paintings of deteriorating walls; scarred and marked by events; textured and weathered; filled with the mysteries of humanity, its celebrations and disappointments both past and present. My goal as an artist is to show how we fit into the world. I try to do this by looking at something man-made that is affected by the passage of time. Walls speak. Hopefully you will never look at one the same way again."

Patricia K. Deaton hails from the foothills of NC. She has lived on Hilton Head Island for 10 years and won a short story contest there in 1993. Her work was published in the Island Packet, in CVCC's 'Sanctuary" and in Woman's World. She loves to be with other writers and belongs to a writers' group on Hilton Head. She attends Beaufort writers' group when possible.

Allan Dehls is retired and living on Dataw Island. In earlier years, primarily in New Hampshire, he specialized in animal portraits on commission.

Kirk Dempsey was born in Beaufort and raised in St. Helena Island. He is married and has two daughters. They live on his family's farm and spend most of their time playing in the shade and selling tomatoes in the summer.

Walter Dennis calls himself "The Dixie Drifter." He lives in Beaufort and says: "I'll write these tales for others to tell, a magnificent greatness. . ." (from his book Stolen Moments).

Diane Britton Dunham, a self-taught artist, says that her creativity comes from within and that she is directed by a Higher Power. "I'm not sure why people love my art so much. The common thread is the simplicity of life. Giving of the heart is the most vulnerable part. It's something offered from the soul."

Nancy Gebhardt moved with her family to Hilton Head Island with the first wave of newcomers and lived there until the late 60s when a career move took the family abroad. Since returning to Hilton Head in 1992, she has published a number of articles and stories including the story on Penn Center, which appeared on the November, 1996 Issue of Beaufort Low Country Magazine.

Dr. Stephen Gordin, a graduate of USC and MUSC, is a practicing radiologist. Originally from Summerton, he fell in love with this area as a child, and moved here about six years ago. He is married, with two stepchildren and two dogs. He enjoys fishing, boating, and golf, is a free-lance writer, and has authored four novels and several short stories.

Scott Gordon developed a love for Beaufort while living in Charleston. He moved here in 1996 to teach Art at BHS. His poems, inspired by being on the water, are verbal records of a visual place within himself. He says they only go as far as words can go. He graduated from USC Columbia, and is published in *The Chronicle* at Clemson University and in USC's Literary Review.

Art Gore was born in Radford, NC in 1926. He served in WWII and in Korea, and worked as a reporter and photographer in Denver before becoming a freelance photographer. He believes that beauty everlasting can whisper and be heard and that everything speaks if only one will pause and listen. Art passed away shortly after donating his work to this project.

Jonathan Green was born in 1955 in Gardens Corner, SC. He graduated from the Art Institute of Chicago in 1982. He is recognized for his style known as "narrative realism" through which he captures and records his early life experiences and the rich cultural heritage of the Gullah Community in which he was raised. His mastery of color and skillful use of the human figure allow him to preserve and share with the viewer a deep sense of community and how the challenges of love, work, and belonging are met.

Annelore Harrell was born and raised in Savannah, GA and spent her summers at her parents' cottage on Myrtle Island. She married a career Army Officer, had five children and traveled from post to post for thirty years. She writes for the *Carolina Morning News,* is a real estate broker, is active in her community, and lives in a river house which she proclaims is just exactly where she wants to be.

Michael Haynes was born in 1966 in Plainfield, NJ and now lives in Bluffton. He is the author of two novels, Sam Patch and Dead River Witch. He truly likes cats, just not the particular two he mentions in his essay.

Lana Hefner was born in Macon, Georgia. She earned her BFA in Interior Design and Painting from the University of Georgia, and pursued both interests until 1992. She now devotes her time exclusively to painting. She has received numerous awards for excellence in painting and her work is found in private and corporate collections throughout the United States and Canada.

Eric Horan is a commercial photographer based in Beaufort, SC. After receiving his degree in Commercial Art & Photography from Colorado Mountain College in 1972, he studied in New York and went on to form his own company.

Eric has traveled extensively and received numerous awards both nationally and internationally for his work.

Akiba Kiiesmira walks a path toward beauty, peace, world harmony, and healing through self-awareness and self-mastery. Artistically she expresses herself through fashion design by combining her philosophies of activism, African Culture, and Spirituality. Her time on St. Helena Island was healing and inspiring.

Arianne King Comer is a Howard University fine arts graduate who moved from Detroit to St. Helena Island in 1994. A United Nations Travel Grant took her to Nigeria to study Yoruba design and indigo dyeing. As a textile artist, Arianne uses traditional and other "resist" techniques to create pieces which have received numerous awards.

Barbara LaPlante received her BA in fine arts from Boston University. She and her husband moved from her native New England to Fripp Island in 1978 where she turned her attention to watercolor painting. She sketches and paints land and seascapes of the Lowcountry. Her prints and note cards may be found in many of the local stores.

Anne Louttit is a native Long Islander who retired from teaching first grade to sail with her husband through the Caribbean and across the South Pacific. After five years on their boat, they settled in Beaufort and have lived on St. Helena Island for eight years. She says "The low country means more to us than we could have dreamed."

Benton Lutz is a licensed family and individual therapist. He speaks at and facilitates seminars and workshops on workplace/employee dynamics, particularly in healthcare settings. A graduate of the College of William and Mary, Presbyterian College, and the Lutheran Theological Seminary at Gettysburg, he is a motivational speaker and published essayist.

Ellen Malphrus, a Low Country native, is currently visiting Assistant Professor of English at USC Beaufort and is *Apostrophe's* fiction editor. Her own fiction and poetry has appeared in many notable publications.

Jacki Martin is a born-again Lowcountry resident who hails from the Midlands of South Carolina. She studied journalism at the University of South Carolina and is director of Public Relations at Technical College of the Lowcountry. Jacki met and fell in love with the Lowcountry and its rivers while working with the Department of Natural Resources.

Lynn McLaren is a resident of Beaufort, SC and a self-employed photojournalist. Her clients include *National Geographic,* The Rockefeller Foundation, *New York Times, Newsweek,* and *Time-Life Books* She was given an Award of Merit by the Government of India for her book *The Village, The People.*

Susan McLendon has been painting for over 25 years. With her husband and 3 daughters, she has lived and worked in Charleston, SC, in Tanzania, Malawi, Grenada, Guatemala, and now in Beaufort. In each location she enjoyed the challenge of finding and painting the essence of the culture.

Wilhelmina Mitchell is an 87year-old retired nurse. Her goal in life is to be able to provide an education for each of her grandchildren.

Jorge A. Otero, a Cuban born photographer, has exhibited extensively throughout the U.S. His work is in private and public collections in the U.S. as well as in Spain, Australia, France, and Colombia. Jorge says: "My photographs are never pre-visualized or pre-planned. They are my perceptions of phenomena, grasped in a fraction of a second, and arranged in a precise order of forms to express the meaning of that instance or event."

Lynda Potter was born and educated in New York State and says Beaufort County is the only place she has ever lived by choice. A lifelong artist, she lived and worked in Florida, Illinois, and Pennsylvania before moving to Bluffton, SC about 10 years ago. She says this area inspires her art like no other place. Potter has had 20 solo shows and her paintings hang in corporate as well as private collections. She won first prize in the 1993 Beaufort Art Association Show.

Nancy Ricker Rhett is a Beaufort native who says: "I paint and write just because I love to and because no one ever told me I couldn't." The Rhett Gallery on Bay Street is popular with locals and tourists alike.

Brewster Milton Robertson is a member of the Southern Book Critics Circle., who has twice been nominated for Best American Essays and the Pushcart Prize. He writes for *Publisher's Weekly* and many national periodicals. Noted for his Fiction Workshops in Beaufort, SC, Brewster founded the Annual Celebration of Writing in the Lowcountry, which is held in Beaufort each summer.

Penny Russell is a snowbird on Fripp Island who taught art in suburban Pittsburgh for 25 years. She graduated from Indiana University of PA and has studied at Penn State and Utah State Universities. During her visits to SC over the years, Penny has participated in several watercolor workshops which have underscored her ties to the Low Country.

Letty Lee Saville was born in Calcutta, India to an American mother and a German father and was raised and educated in Europe. Her favorite medium is watercolor, but she also works in acrylics and oil. She enjoys tennis, flower arranging, gardening, and crafts. She moved with her husband to Beaufort 18 years ago.

Doris Schrock - Sunlight dancing across ancient oaks, patent sheen of green magnolia leaf, salt tides and pelican wings, eddying mists of folklore, all fingering bright echoes in my pots of paints. (by Sharon E. McGee)

Barbara Shipman moved to Beaufort in 1976 and took art classes to capture the Lowcountry. She received her highest honor in 1982 when her original watercolor, "Coconut Palm," was included in the American Watercolor Society's 127th Annual International Exhibit. Shipman Gallery on Bay Street has been "must see" since its opening in 1995.

Carolyn C. Smith and her husband are natives of Bluffton. Carolyn has written for the *Bluffton Packet* and is an active member of Bluffton United Methodist Church. If you go to All Joy Beach and see Carolyn or her family on the porch of the Tall Chimney, stop and say hello, or wave as you pass.

Joan Templer was born in South Africa where she earned her BA in Fine Arts and received considerable recognition as a painter. She came to the US with her husband and two daughters in 1969 when she attended Columbia University in New York. The family then moved to Atlanta where she and her husband taught at the GA Tech. College of Architecture for 20 years. Since moving to Beaufort, Ms. Templer received first prize in the Beaufort Art Association's Spring Exhibit.

Sheila Tombe is a native of Belfast, Northern Ireland and has lived in Beaufort since 1993. She is currently an associate professor of English at USC Beaufort where she edits *Apostrophe.*

Ethard W. Van Stee is a veteran actor, and a writer of an historical biography, one and 1/2 novels and several plays. A member of the Beaufort Writers Association from its inception, he inherited its directorship following the untimely death of its founder, Chris Heles.

Laura Von Harten was born in Texas where her parents were shrimping and moved to her father's hometown of Beaufort when she was very young. She spent her first five years living above the family fish market on Lady's Island. Laura teaches Anthropology at USC-Beaufort and is working on a documentary and a book about the seafood industries.

Nancy Easter White earned her MFA in Historic Preservation from Savannah College of Art & Design, with a specialization in photography. She shoots commercially using a large format camera to document architectural features. Her fine art photography evokes the southern vernacular and its cultural icons.

Index